RIDICULOUS FAITH!

Ordinary People Living Extraordinary Lives

— Shundrawn A. Thomas —

DESTINY IMAGE® PUBLISHERS, INC.

P.O. Box 310, Shippensburg, PA 17257-0310

*"Speaking to the Purposes of God for This Generation
and for the Generations to Come."*

This book and all other Destiny Image, Revival Press, MercyPlace, Fresh Bread, Destiny Image Fiction, and Treasure House books are available at Christian bookstores and distributors worldwide.

For a U.S. bookstore nearest you, call 1-800-722-6774.

For more information on foreign distributors, call 717-532-3040.

Or reach us on the Internet:
www.destinyimage.com

ISBN 10: 0-7684-2355-4

ISBN 13: 978-0-7684-2355-6

For Worldwide Distribution, Printed in the U.S.A.

1 2 3 4 5 6 7 8 9 10 11 / 10 09 08 07 06

DEDICATION

This book is dedicated to Abraham, the father of faith. Through obedience he inherited the promises of God, even the promise that his seed would inherit the earth. This book is dedicated to every believer courageous enough to live by faith. In spirit we are Abraham's seed and joint heirs with Christ, the seed in whom the promise is fulfilled. We are the offspring of God and rulers in the earth according to His promise.

ACKNOWLEDGMENTS

First, I give praise to my Lord and Savior, Jesus Christ, for the gift of abundant life. In all endeavors I acknowledge Him because He directs my path.

To Latania, and our sons, Javon and Micah. I thank you for your perfect love and your unfaltering support. Latania, you have helped me to believe that with God all things are possible. Our family is truly blessed.

To my pastors and parents, Gary and Audrey Thomas. The just do live by faith. You have taught me that in words and deeds.

To my siblings, Michael, Jarreon, and Saeyonniea. As for our house, we have decided to serve the Lord. Continue to contend for the faith.

To my friend and business partner, Cliff, and your lovely wife, Janelle. Keep stepping out in faith and allowing God to do the seemingly impossible in your life.

To my extended family—the Thomas family, the Austin and Brandon families, the Alleyne family, and the Look Up & Live Full Gospel family. Thank you for believing in me.

To the men and women of God who have encouraged me to live by faith. The late Maimie Till Mobley, the late Pastor George Liggins, Dr. Myles Munroe, Pastors Carlton and Paul Arthurs, Dr. John Cherry, Pastor Bill Hybels, Pastor Kirbyjohn Caldwell, Dr. Fred Price, Pastor Ben Gibert, Pastor Michael Hurst, Pastor Rick Warren, Pastor Jim Cymbala, John Eldredge, Elder Isaac Greene, Elder Theadius Toney, Rev. Anne Marie Mingo, Minister Maxine Walker, Rev. Andre LaNier, Michael Young, and Jwyanza Nuriddin. God bless you.

To everyone who purchases this book. May you be enlightened and encouraged as you fight the good fight of faith.

TABLE OF CONTENTS

PART I:
A FRESH PERSPECTIVE

PART II:
TAKING INVENTORY

PREFACE

For therein is the righteousness of God revealed from faith to faith: as it is written, The just shall live by faith (Romans 1:17 KJV).

The Bible is literally full of accounts of seemingly ordinary people who accomplished extraordinary things. While the scenery, timing, or particulars changed, one aspect remained consistent. Individuals differing little from you or me enjoyed great success or experienced great failure based on their faith in God. One could argue that's what the Bible is all about—faith in God. One could also argue that the most important charge of every believer is to live by faith.

For years I attempted to grab hold of the charge to live by faith. I read about faith, confessed faith, and followed the commonly accepted convictions regarding how faith works. I maintained a positive outlook. I felt good about my relationship with God, and I felt good about myself. Nonetheless, I failed to realize many of the promises of God on a consistent basis.

I pressed on. I knew what the Word said concerning me, and it was high time I stepped out in faith. So step out I did. I made bold statements and backed them up with bold actions. My statements did not alter my reality. As for my bold actions...well, they were definitively bold, but seemingly ineffective. The result was frustration, confusion, and doubt—frustration with my circumstances, confusion regarding my purpose, and doubt with respect to my relationship with God. Everyone else was naming it and laying claim to it, weren't they?

Maybe you've experienced similar feelings. If you have, I can assure you that you're not alone. If you haven't, just keep living! I've come to accept that in my walk with God, fear and doubt are ever present. They are not character flaws; they are emotions. They are emotions that arise because there is very real opposition to the plan God has for my life. The very presence of these emotions places demands on my faith. But I've found that when I conquer my greatest opposition— manifested as my own doubts and fears—I can actually accomplish things I once believed impossible.

The Bible declares that righteous men and women live by faith. Yet even the great patriarch Abraham, known to many as the father of faith, encountered instances where his faith failed. Have you encountered such times in your life? Perhaps the better question is this: How often do you encounter such times in your life? It is during trying times that faith is put to the test. It is when we run out of rational possibilities that faith comes into focus.

Faith is not exemplified by confidence in God's ability to do the things we know are possible. Rather it is demonstrated by our confidence in God's ability to do those things that are seemingly impossible. Faith is relying on God to do those things that He has reserved especially for Himself—those things He alone can accomplish. Faith brings everything within our reach because God extends our reach.

Time and time again, the Bible gives us the example of everyday people going beyond what they or others thought possible due to their faith in God. For years I read about these everyday people, but the truth is, I never viewed them as everyday people. While I never doubted the stories were true, the characters simply weren't real to me. By that, I mean I couldn't identify with them. I could readily see their spiritual attributes, but I could scarcely appreciate their human attributes. The characters were great subject matter for Sunday's sermon, but they were not practical examples that I could use in my everyday life. While reading the story of David for what seemed like the hundredth time, God spoke to me.

He told me that I needed to change my perspective. He showed me that my challenge in the area of faith was not a lack of understanding, but a misunderstanding. I had processed many of the stories and characters of the Bible in the wrong way. I had looked past the human element for a formula and a rational approach to faith. I was searching the Scriptures for a step-by-step guide rather than seeing the unique ways that God deals with real people.

That day, God began to change my perspective. Now when I examine the great men and women of the Bible, I take a different approach. I look first for their human elements and traits. I examine how God worked with their unique personalities, abilities, and situations. I see them for their spirituality, and I see them for their greatness. But just as important, I see their hopes, fears, strengths, and weaknesses. I see them as spirit, and I see them as special. Most of all, I see them as real people. In essence, I see them the way God sees them—and the way He sees me.

By changing my perspective of the Bible, God has revealed the essence of faith in a way I hadn't seen before. In turn, my faith has increased and my relationship with Him has been fortified. With this in mind, I purposed in my heart to write this book. My desire is simply to share my unique perspective of faith. I do not consider my vantage point as that of a man who has traveled to some far place in God never seen before, but rather the perspective of a fellow traveler on this pilgrim journey.

God is performing and will continue to perform the seemingly impossible in my life. The wonderful thing about God is that He can, will, and likely is doing the same for you. God has something great in store for all those who trust Him. It is up to us to uncover the treasure He has placed within us. To others who do not share our conviction, the dreams God places in our heart seem, in a word, *ridiculous*. I want to encourage you by declaring that God has equipped you with the perfect something that you need in order to overcome the criticisms of others and the doubts that emanate from within you. That something is what I like to refer to as *Ridiculous Faith*.

Introduction

The Lord who delivered me from the paw of the lion and the paw of the bear will deliver me from the hand of this Philistine (1 Samuel 17:37a NIV).

The epitome of *Ridiculous Faith* is demonstrated in the account of David's victory over Goliath. The story is set around 1020 B.C. The nation of Israel had been at war with opposing nations since entering the Canaan land. The Philistines were longstanding rivals who constantly opposed Israel. The Israelites feared the Philistines and had repeatedly cried out to God for deliverance from their bitter enemies. The appointment of Saul as the first king of Israel was in direct response to the cry of the people for a king to serve as their champion and deliverer (see 1 Sam. 8:19-20).

The Philistines had gathered their army in the hills just west of the Valley of Elah, which was located between the hill country of Judah and the lowlands of the Philistines. Saul countered by gathering his troops on the east hills of the Valley of Elah. As the battle lines were drawn and the armies were set to engage one another, a champion named Goliath came out of the Philistine ranks.

Goliath was a towering figure, who stood approximately nine feet, nine inches tall. The Bible records that his coat of scale armor weighed 125 pounds and his spearhead alone weighed 15 pounds. Goliath issued a challenge to the army of Israel. He said that the army of Israel should choose a man to meet him in combat. If the Israelite prevailed, the Philistines would serve the nation of Israel. If Goliath prevailed, the Israelites would serve the Philistines.

For 40 days, morning and evening, Goliath issued his challenge. Each day Goliath would come out from the Philistine ranks to shout at his opponents, and when he issued his challenge, the Israelite army would literally run away in fear. In an effort to find a challenger, King Saul offered a great reward to any man who killed Goliath. Specifically he offered riches, exemption from taxes, and his daughter's hand in marriage. However, despite the king's offer, no man was willing to accept the challenge.

A DATE WITH DESTINY

The challenge issued by Goliath represented a pivotal point in the destiny of two men. Prior to David's arrival on the scene, many able-bodied men shrank in fear when facing the enemy, and despite God's faithfulness to Israel, no man was willing to accept the challenge. Goliath, who embodied the opposition, simply loomed larger than the promises and provision of God. While anyone among the ranks of Israel could have accepted the challenge, the Bible clearly depicts that one man was uniquely suited.

Many people overlook the subtle yet important fact that this was initially Saul's date with destiny—not David's. Let's examine Saul's resume. Saul was of the tribe of Benjamin, a tribe known for their courage and exploits in war. You could say that fighting was in his blood. Though he was smaller than Goliath, he was a full head taller than the other Israelites. Saul was a proven warrior who had personally led Israel to numerous military conquests. Most importantly, it was prophesied of Saul that he would deliver Israel from the hand of the Philistines (see 1 Sam. 9:16). Saul had the pedigree and the promise, yet there was one small problem—he didn't trust God. The absence of faith nullifies the promises of God. Saul succumbed to his fears and forfeited the destiny that God intended for him.

I learned an important lesson as I examined the life of Saul. Fear will overtake your destiny if you allow it. Your destiny is not guaranteed because God cannot override your will. Destiny is simply God's preferred or desired end for you. God reveals his plan or destiny for your life, but it is only through faith that it is manifested. I also learned that I can't avoid the tests God allows in my life. Just as Goliath emerged daily to defy Saul and his army, my tests will come until I overcome them or they overcome me.

THE MAN IN THE MIDDLE

While others may be reluctant to admit it, I can identify with Saul. At times, I've allowed fear or anxiety to get the best of me despite my assurances from God. While we all hope to have triumphant experiences like David's victory over Goliath, we will almost assuredly have Saul-like failures that set us back. Success is often birthed in failure. There will always be a seemingly insurmountable obstacle standing between you and your destiny. In Saul's case, the obstacle was Goliath. Saul lost the battle in his heart and subsequently never made it to the battlefield.

Faith is the prerequisite for completing the assignment God has given you. This is because God gives us all an assignment that lies just beyond our human capabilities. God takes us into clear and present danger and allows us to stare fear in the face. It is at these pivotal times that we draw on our faith and in doing so draw closer to God. Goliath represents the obstacles we face on the way to our destiny. We are guaranteed victory if we stand on the Word of God. Conversely, we forfeit our victory when we move our focus from the prize to the problem. Our obstacles are only as big as the space we allow them to occupy in our hearts and minds. God promises to give us perfect peace when we keep our thoughts continually on Him (see Isa. 26:3). When

His Word becomes our preoccupation, the prize is always greater than the problem.

THE REPLACEMENT

As Saul's story was transpiring, there was a parallel story unfolding concerning David, the son of Jesse. Jesse lived in Bethlehem with his family, which included eight sons. David, the youngest of Jesse's sons, was a handsome young man with a kind heart and a pleasant disposition. While he served as caretaker of his father's sheep, his three eldest brothers served in Saul's army. Serving in the army was a position that brought with it prestige and respect; however, shepherding was the occupation that God initially chose to develop His future king.

One day, Jesse instructed David to carry a supply of food to his brothers as well as the captain of their unit. When David arrived on the scene, he found the morale of his fellow countrymen to be extremely low. For 40 days the Philistine champion had taunted the nation of Israel with his challenge, and David witnessed firsthand the shame of the Israelite army, literally fleeing from the presence of Goliath. After Goliath returned to the Philistine ranks, several men in the camp discussed the reward Saul promised to anyone who killed Goliath. Others were paralyzed by fear, but David began to inquire about the reward offered by Saul.

Consider this: An entire army of battle-tested men had heard the same challenge and every one of them continued to focus on the problem. Then, an unassuming young shepherd hears the same challenge and immediately focuses on the prize. How you see the world is determined by the condition of your heart. God always has a reward stored up for us on the other side of our tests. Those who walk in faith learn to look past the challenge and focus on the reward. In Chapter 16 we will examine this idea more closely.

TALKING LOUD

So David began to speak to the men in the camp concerning the "uncircumcised Philistine" and then proclaimed that he would fight

Goliath and remove the disgrace from Israel. David's oldest brother, Eliab, became angry when he heard David's courageous words. His anger was likely born out of his own fears and the jealousy that he harbored for his younger brother. Prior to the account of David's victory over Goliath, the Bible records Samuel anointing David in the midst of his brothers. I've often wondered if David's family was aware that he was being anointed as the next king of Israel, for the Bible appears silent on this point. It is clear that Samuel was consecrating David for an important office; nonetheless, he likely concealed the nature of David's appointment at that time.

Despite the criticism of his brother, David continued to speak in faith. The Bible tells us that he was repeatedly outspoken in his resolve that a Philistine should not defy the army of the living God. He spoke with such confidence that his words were conveyed to Saul. There is a principle at work here. Look at it this way: David spoke in faith, and his testimony was made known to the king. When you speak in faith, your testimony is made known to the King. Saul eventually sent for David as a result of his conviction. Isn't that a wonderful example? We all should aspire to speak with such conviction. Our confession gives the King of kings the right to intervene in our lives.

When David informed Saul that he was willing and able to fight Goliath, Saul initially dismissed David's request because of his youth and lack of fighting experience. He essentially told David that he didn't have a chance going up against a proven warrior the likes of Goliath. Saul's response is typical of what we hear from individuals faced with adversity. People regularly project their own fears on others. If they can't envision themselves accomplishing a feat, they readily assume others will also fail. Yet David did not waver in the midst Saul's doubts, and he refused to let Saul upset the condition of his heart. Listen to his response to Saul's opinion:

> ... Your servant has been keeping his father's sheep. When a lion or a bear came and carried off a sheep from the flock, I went after it, struck it and rescued the sheep from its mouth. When it turned on me, I seized it by its hair, struck it and killed it. Your servant has killed both

the lion and the bear; this uncircumcised Philistine will be like one of them, because he has defied the armies of the living God (1 Samuel 17:34-36 NIV).

God prepared David, while he was in the pasture, for combat, not while he was on the battlefield. He knew that David's encounter with Goliath would require more than his natural abilities. David's experience with the lion and the bear conditioned him to trust in God rather than his own abilities, and he had confidence that the same God who gave him power over a lion and a bear would give him victory over Goliath—no matter how intimidating his opponent appeared.

TAILOR-MADE

David's courage and conviction compelled Saul to yield to his request to fight the Philistine champion. Here, we must not overlook the significance of Saul's actions at this juncture. The Israelite who accepted the challenge would carry the fate of the nation with him. Recall Goliath's challenge—he declared that the loser's nation should become the servants of the victor's nation. The outcome of the fight would undoubtedly impact the morale of the respective armies and the outcome of the overall conflict.

Saul dressed David in his own garments and outfitted him with a coat of armor, helmet, and sword. At this point, David made an interesting declaration. He stated that he could not go into battle with the customary armor and sword because he had not proven them. He felt uncomfortable going into battle with tools that were foreign to him. The Bible informs us that David removed the armor and put aside the sword. He then opted for his staff, sling, and five smooth stones, which he placed in his shepherd's bag. Think of how absurd David's actions must have appeared to the ranks of Israel's army that were present. David, armed with only a staff and sling, was going to engage presumably the most feared warrior of that time. I imagine there were those who attempted to dissuade him from this course of action, yet David obviously stood firm in his resolve.

We must examine David's statement closely. Many incorrectly surmise that the armor did not fit David because it was too big and cumbersome for him to wear. However, this is not what Scripture tells us. Some people picture David as a small boy, which I believe was not the case. David was a youth or young man. Saul's reference to his youth speaks more to his lack of military experience than his age. Bear in mind that David initially put on the tunic, armor, and sword but quickly realized that it was unwise to go to battle with weapons he'd never tested. In David's plea to Saul, he mentioned his conquests as a shepherd. His weapons were his staff and his sling. Those things were the weaponry he was familiar with and the weaponry he had success with. More importantly, they were the tools that God made use of in aiding David in his exploits. David had proven his staff and sling and, more importantly, he'd proven God. His trust in his staff and sling were symbolic of his faith in God.

There is an important lesson to be learned here. God fully equips us for the destiny that He sets before us. We must have confidence in His promise as well as His provision. Those around David likely assumed his provisions were inadequate, and David may have entertained these thoughts for a short time. But after careful consideration, David went to battle with the same equipment he arrived with. As ridiculous as it may have seemed to others, he was perfectly equipped to walk in victory. We must have the same confidence in God. We should not covet the gifts, abilities, or possessions of others. God has furnished each one of us with exactly what we need to complete our destiny in the earth. We maintain our confidence by looking to God and not people for affirmation.

EVERYDAY HEROES

I've heard many sermons regarding David and Goliath, but what I find intriguing is that I've never heard the suggestion that David may have been fearful. I picture David descending into the Valley of Elah, and I wonder about the thoughts going through his mind. I may be in a minority, but I believe it is likely that David dealt with fear. I have trouble believing that satan would have let this significant accomplishment go unchallenged.

In the modern-day church we tend to sensationalize faith. The accounts are depicted in such a way that they no longer seem achievable. Faith does not permanently displace fear; it's what we rely on to overcome our feelings of fear or inadequacy. I believe David engaged in an internal struggle before actually facing Goliath. Viewed this way, his testimony is much more encouraging. It demonstrates that David not only conquered Goliath, but he conquered his fears as well. David's famous Psalm comes to mind. "Even though I walk through the valley of the shadow of death, I have overcome my fear, because God is with me" (Ps. 23:4, author's paraphrase)

When Goliath set eyes on David, he despised him. He didn't believe David was worthy of engaging him in battle, and he attempted to arouse fear within David by issuing idle threats. David responded by professing his confidence in God's ability to give him victory over his opponent. David understood that he was in covenant with the true living God, and he concluded with the famous statement that the battle is the Lord's. His profession of faith opened the door for God to intercede on his behalf.

After his bold declaration of faith, the Bible states that David literally leaped into action. As he ran to engage Goliath, he reached for his simple yet proven weapon. With one fatal sling of a stone, David landed a blow that brought down Goliath. True to his profession, he beheaded Goliath—with Goliath's own sword no less. David's courageous act discouraged the Philistines, who fled in fear, and encouraged his countrymen, who hotly pursued them. That day the nation of Israel spoiled the Philistines of many of their possessions, all because of the courageous act of one unlikely hero. David earned and received a victor's reward. However, God received the glory. This is the result that faith always produces when called upon.

The story of David and Goliath demonstrates that heroes come in all shapes and sizes. In other words, real heroes are everyday people like you and me. God was not concerned about David's physical appearance or social status. His Word teaches that the true measure of an individual is determined by the condition of his heart (see 1 Sam. 16:7). I pray that this introduction has conditioned your heart to receive my message concerning *Ridiculous Faith*. I also pray that this book will encourage you as you live the extraordinary life that God has destined for you.

Part I
A Fresh Perspective

A Fresh Perspective

Now faith is the substance of things hoped for, the evidence of things not seen (Hebrews 11:1 KJV).

What is the essence of faith? An inspired writer's words were immortalized when he described faith as the assurance of something we hope for but do not yet see. While meditating on this familiar verse, I came to a simple realization. Faith is the full-grown offspring of hope. Over time I've ascribed to a paradigm identifying three progressive levels of trust. There is hope, followed by belief, concluding with faith. This continuum applies generally to our trust in God and specifically to our reliance on His Word.

Hope is the anticipation of a favorable outcome and is closely tied to your desires. Hope signifies what you want God to perform on your behalf. Hope is often inspired by the favorable experiences of others. When you observe something good happen to someone else, it gives you hope that you can enjoy a similar experience. That is why your testimony is so important. It ignites hope in the hearts of others. The relationship I have with my employer provides a practical example of hope. I joined my current employer based largely on the firm's outstanding reputation as well as my recruitment by current tenured employees. I hope to enjoy a rewarding career with the firm, and I am encouraged by the testimony of those who have preceded me.

Belief goes beyond hope. Belief is confidence in the ability of another. Belief is generally based on firsthand knowledge or experience. Belief is established when you are convinced of God's ability to perform His Word. Belief is what you personally know God can perform on your behalf. The relationship that we have with our family physician provides a practical example of belief. Our family has been blessed with good health, but there have been occasions over the years where we have required medical attention. During these occasions we have visited with our trusted practitioner. We have great confidence in her knowledge, training, and skill; and because of our experience with her over the years, we believe in her ability to help our condition.

Faith is the final step on our continuum. It is not based on what you want, nor is it predicated on your experiences *per se*. Faith is the reliance you have on the words and intentions of another. Faith is based solely on your relationship with God. It is what you fully expect God to do on your behalf. However, the exercise of faith does not mean you always get your desired outcome. True faith is the courage to act with only the assurance that the one you have placed your faith in will do what is best for you. The relationship I share with my young children provides a practical example of faith. My two boys are fond of jumping off things into my waiting arms. Sometimes this occurs without much warning. They don't simply *believe* that I will catch them; they fully *expect* me to. Their unfeigned faith is demonstrated by their willingness to act based solely on our relationship.

In our exploration of faith, we will regularly refer to this paradigm. Along the way we will examine the lives of several well-known and other lesser known biblical characters. As we draw insight from their experiences, we will witness time and again how an interaction with Christ Jesus transforms lives from ordinary to extraordinary. I will also use this framework to share personal challenges, trials, and triumphs from my own walk of faith.

In the first section of the book, we will apply our paradigm to take a fresh look at faith and its role in the human life. In doing so, I pray that God broadens your perspective of faith in much the same way that He has expanded mine. Ultimately, I believe that this journey will lead us all to the same conclusion. God's greatest desire is to develop a personal and practical relationship with each one of us. The exercise of faith is not about miracles *per se*. The exercise of faith is not about the acquisition of material things. The exercise of faith is our bold expression of our unwavering trust in God our Father. Let's begin our exploration of *Ridiculous Faith*.

Chapter 1

A Long Time Coming

And we rejoice in the hope of the glory of God. Not only so, but we also rejoice in our sufferings, because we know that suffering produces perseverance; perseverance, character; and character, hope. And hope does not disappoint us, because God has poured out His love into our hearts by the Holy Spirit, whom He has given us (Romans 5:2b-5 NIV).

Paul the apostle is regarded as one of the greatest evangelists and teachers of all time. His Spirit-filled letters admonish and encourage believers who seek to grow in faith and develop a lasting relationship with God. Paul's letter to the assembly of believers at Rome is widely considered his most compelling and complete epistle. It is interesting to note that Paul penned this letter prior to visiting Rome. Paul had received word of the spread of the Gospel in Rome and wrote his letter to exhort his fellow believers until he had the occasion to visit them.

The theme of hope is prominent throughout his letter. This topic was not foreign to Paul. Recall that he is the same inspired writer who described faith as assurance of what we hope for but do not yet see. Paul explained that we should rejoice in the hope of God's Kingdom. He expounded that this type of hope gives joy and leads to success. It also brings with it the expectation that something wonderful will happen when God's will becomes the meditation of our heart.

Hope is the spark in the soul of an individual that ignites the flame of faith. Paul intuitively understood the vital need for hope in the human life. In fact, Paul talked about hope more than any other contributor to the Bible. Paul's letter encourages us never to lose hope. It reassures us that if we simply maintain our hope in God, He will not disappoint us. Paul does not mislead his audience; he warns that we will face adversity. It is through adversity that we build character. Moreover, it is through adversity that our hope matures into full grown faith.

Is There a Doctor in the House?

Jesus saith unto him, Rise, take up thy bed, and walk (John 5:8 KJV).

The temple in Jerusalem was the backdrop for many notable events recorded in the New Testament of the Bible. During the time of Jesus' ministry, there was a pool called Bethesda located just outside the temple. This pool had become a gathering post for a great number of disabled people. Among these were the blind, lame, paralyzed, and those with any number of afflictions. They gathered by the pool of Bethesda because it was a place where miracles took place. During a particular time of year, an angel went into the pool and stirred up the water. The first person to make it into the pool once the water was stirred was cured of their affliction.

To me, the scene appears ironic. At the epicenter of Jerusalem you have the temple symbolizing the presence of the living God. Just outside that temple you have a multitude of disabled people. I am reminded of the words of the prophet Jeremiah. "Is there no balm in Gilead? Is there no physician there?" It also makes me think of the modern-day houses of worship that pepper the urban and rural landscape. Masses lie just outside our ubiquitous sanctuaries. They urgently need a physician. They too are desperately seeking miracles.

Unbeknownst to the multitude outside the temple, there was a chief physician in their midst. Jesus had just arrived on the scene. I wonder what His itinerary was that day. Maybe He was on His way to the temple, or maybe He was returning from worship. Maybe He was led by the Spirit to that particular place. Whatever the case, one unsuspecting individual was scheduled for a divine appointment.

BEDRIDDEN

Among the multitude was a man who'd been plagued with an illness for 38 years. The specific nature of his illness is not clear, but the account suggests that the illness rendered him very weak and likely crippled. In fact, his illness confined him to a pallet that he used for a bed. There he lay among the multitude hoping for a miracle. How many years had he come to that site? How many times had he witnessed others receive the miracle he desperately hoped for?

In my opinion, this unnamed man's story is a perfect example of hope. Despite years of suffering with an infirmity and years of disappointment, one thing is clear—he kept coming back! While he may not be the ideal example of faith or even belief, he sustained hope. Despite his broken condition, he held out for a miracle.

The Bible tells us that Jesus noticed this man. Among a multitude of sick and disabled people, this one man stuck out. Why did Jesus notice him? Healing any one of the multitude present would have constituted a miracle. Indeed, had He chosen to, He could have healed everyone present that day. (There are accounts recorded in the Bible where He did just that.) However, on this day, the focus was one man.

As I alluded before, God does not view people with the same biases we do. God focuses on the condition of the heart. I can't help but believe that there was something about the condition of that man's heart that prepared him for a miracle. I'm not suggesting that he was in some way more deserving of a miracle. I simply mean that the hope that was alive in his heart made him a candidate for a miraculous change.

Bedside Manner

While it is true that Jesus perceived or had foreknowledge of many things, we should be careful not to overlook the personal nature of this meeting. It is reasonable to believe that Jesus learned of the nature and length of his condition during the course of a conversation. This was one way that He demonstrated compassion. He regularly spent time with the types of people whom many of us ignore.

Jesus may have visited the temple with the express purpose of healing the invalid man, or maybe He simply decided to heal him during the course of their conversation. Whatever the case, His compassion was moved to action when He offered the man the miracle he'd hoped for. Here, we observe the Chief Physician going to work. We also observe something curious about His methods. Jesus began by asking what we might consider a rhetorical question. "Do you want to get well?"

This man was likely surprised by the question. After all, Jesus knew he'd been sick for 38 years. The man responded by explaining that in times past, no one availed themselves to help him into the pool; subsequently, he was never the first person into the water. The pool was his focus, his failures from the past were a preoccupation, and a lack of assistance was seen as an impediment. Yet Jesus was poised to give him an instruction that would change his life, and He began by shifting the man's focus.

With no mention of the pool and no reference to his past, Jesus instructed him to pick up his bed and walk. Jesus did not assist him nor did He treat him as an invalid. You don't tell a disabled man to get up by himself! He treated the man like an individual who was physically whole, and that is just how the man responded. Without assistance and without hesitation, the man picked up his pallet and departed in perfect health.

The Sabbath Police

I can picture the man making his way through the crowd of sick and disabled people, carrying the pallet that symbolized the sickness that had bound him for years. This man was likely rejoicing in his heart, but he would soon discover that not everyone was overjoyed for him. It so happened that the miracle in question took place on the Sabbath. The Bible records that the man encountered certain religious leaders or teachers of the law who apparently stopped the man to chastise him and inform him that it was unlawful to carry his bed on the Sabbath. For 38 years this man had struggled to complete even the simplest tasks. Finally, Jesus had freed him from his bed of affliction, but religious leaders preferred to confine him to it based on a technicality.

Mosaic Law did require Jews to refrain from any type of work on the Sabbath (see Ex. 20:8-10); however, over time the religious leaders mixed numerous traditions with the law, and by Jesus' day, they had 39 definitions for work, which apparently included carrying a pallet. There was even debate over whether an individual could wear a wooden leg or use artificial teeth. When the law enforcement agents questioned the man about his supposed infraction, he informed them that his unidentified physician had instructed him to carry his bed. Although the keepers of the law suggested that the law had been broken, Jesus' instructions never caused the man to break God's law; Jesus simply broke with tradition.

Those who chastised the man were guilty of the same trespasses of many modern-day religious practitioners. Their practice overshadowed their purpose. Religion or religious practices depict how we choose to serve God. Religion is not inherently bad. In fact, James discusses pure religion in his Epistle to the early Church (see James 1:27). Nevertheless, God requires worship and not religion. Religious traditions can diminish your hope in God if you're not careful. Therefore, you must always stand ready to change your opinions and actions to align yourself with God's will. That's what hope is all about—the possibility that your circumstances will change. It is the thought in your heart, no matter how distant, that God will turn a situation in your favor.

HOPE SPRINGS ETERNAL

This story has an interesting ending. After his run-in with the authorities, the man proceeded to the temple. He may have gone to

33

worship, thankful for the miracle he'd received. But whatever his reason, the Bible informs us that Jesus found the man in the temple. The language implies that Jesus did not chance upon him. In fact, the word used in the original Greek suggests the second meeting was the result of a purposeful search (see John 5:14).

Jesus had withdrawn from the multitude at the pool because He perceived the hatred of those who were plotting against Him. He was well aware that healing on the Sabbath would cause a ruckus, and this is perhaps the real reason that He didn't heal the others at the pool. Jesus searched for the man so that He could deliver an essential message. Jesus told His patient to stop sinning or something worse might happen to him. With this instruction Jesus departed, having also revealed His identity.

This story teaches us a profound lesson. Hope alone does not change your circumstances. It is an elementary step on the way to faith. It has been said that this man was healed without exercising faith, and several details of the account seem to support this viewpoint. At the time of his healing, this man had no idea who Jesus was. He didn't even have an opportunity to thank Jesus before He slipped away in the crowd. Nonetheless, I view the interaction in a slightly different way. I think that Jesus perceived the hope that resided in the man's heart and spoke a word that caused him to believe. The man responded with an act of faith, albeit a simple one. The man was healed because Jesus gave him assurance of what he'd hoped for.

Jesus' purpose for becoming a man was to restore our severed relationship with our Father. He is not only the hope of Israel, but the hope of the whole world. His first order of business was to deal with sin. The man healed at Bethesda was unaware that his real problem was sin. The disability was merely a symptom. By identifying Himself, Jesus revealed where the man's hope should lie. The man didn't have to place his hope in a pool if his hope was in Christ Jesus. For it is only in Christ Jesus that we have the hope of eternal life.

Remember, hope is a precursor to faith. When Jesus Christ becomes the focus of our hope, we are well on our way to exhibiting

Ridiculous Faith. (This will be further discussed in Chapter 4.) Hope is essential to coping with trying times. It is said that a thousand-mile journey begins with one step. Likewise, our eternal walk with God begins with hope in the redemptive power of His Son, Christ Jesus.

Chapter 2

Help My Unbelief!

Just believe that I am in the Father and the Father is in Me. Or at least believe because of what you have seen Me do. The truth is, anyone who believes in Me will do the same works I have done, and even greater works, because I am going to be with the Father (John 14:11-12 NLT).

In the Gospel of John, we read a detailed account of Christ's last supper with His disciples. Partway through the evening, Philip asked Jesus to show them the Father, and declared that if Jesus would show them the Father, they would be satisfied. Philip's request was in response to Jesus' promise to prepare a place for them and to receive them at a future date, and Philip implied that if Jesus showed them the Father, they would believe Him. The question revealed a serious shortcoming within Philip as well as the other disciples. For although they shared an intimate relationship with Jesus, they still harbored unbelief.

Phillip's question deeply affected Jesus. He marveled that Philip still did not know Him despite all the time they'd spent together, and He told Philip that he should have at least been persuaded by the miracles he witnessed. Jesus hadn't simply proclaimed the power of the Kingdom of God, but He demonstrated it as well. Jesus then admonished Philip that if he or anyone else believes in Him, they can perform the same miracles He performed and even greater wonders. The ultimate objective was to bring glory to the Father.

Every one of us is destined for great works; nevertheless, miraculous change must be preceded by belief. It is our belief in the ability of God to perform His word that infuses the supernatural into our everyday lives. As we stated earlier, belief is generally the product of firsthand knowledge or experience. We establish our belief by searching the Word of God and seeking His presence daily. It is through this intimacy that we come to know Him and trust that He will do just what He promises.

UNINVITED GUEST

Jesus said unto him, If thou canst believe, all things are possible to him that believeth (Mark 9:23 KJV).

Oftentimes, Jesus would venture into the mountains to spend time in prayer and meditation, and on one particular occasion, He took Peter, James, and John with Him to witness His transfiguration. When Jesus returned to the other disciples, He found them surrounded by a crowd and arguing with teachers of the law. He then demanded to know why His disciples were being questioned, and a man among the crowd responded to Jesus' inquiry.

This man informed Jesus that his son was possessed by an evil spirit, which rendered the child speechless. What's more, the evil spirit would seize the boy and cause him to behave erratically. The desperate father, wanting nothing more than to see his son delivered and having hoped in the testimony of Jesus' authority over evil spirits, brought his son to the disciples. The disciples did attempt to cast out the evil spirit but were unsuccessful, which seems to have sparked the debate and led to the commotion.

Jesus' initial response appears to reflect disappointment more than compassion, because He describes those present as a faithless people. While His remarks applied to all present, He particularly chastised His defeated disciples. Notice that Jesus tied their inability to drive out the evil spirit to their lack of faith. The proper application of faith was necessary to address the man's problem.

Although disappointed and seemingly frustrated with those around Him, Jesus still exercised compassion when He instructed them to bring the boy so that He could tend to him. Jesus never viewed people as an inconvenience. Regardless of His physical or emotional condition, He made people a priority. And so, they quickly brought the youth in order for Jesus to examine him.

When the resident evil spirit saw Jesus, it immediately threw the boy into a violent convulsion. The boy began wallowing and foaming at the mouth, just as the father had described. It was as if the evil spirit wanted to demonstrate that it was in control. I imagine that this sight must have startled many of those present; however, there is no sign that Jesus was troubled one bit. Instead, He continued His dialogue with the father, further inquiring about the boy's condition.

The father explained that his son had been possessed since childhood, and the spirit had often cast the boy into fire or water in an attempt to end his life. This account makes me think about the craftiness of the devil. He too seeks to take up residence in our lives. He tempts us with sin, and once bound, we act out of character. His objective is to separate us from God. This boy had the same fundamental need we all share. He needed the freedom gained through the redemptive power of Christ Jesus. For those whom He makes free, are free indeed (see John 8:36).

WHEN TWO WORLDS COLLIDE

Discussing his son's condition must have evoked painful emotions for the man. He was powerless over his son's affliction, which had to be very disheartening for a father. He had likely already sought countless others for an answer to his problem and even called upon the disciples prior to speaking with Jesus. At this point, his desperate search had likely taken its toll. While he believed there was an answer, his experiences had dampened his faith. He finally asked Jesus to have pity on them and help them if He could. Jesus then explained that anything is possible if a person believes (see Mark 9:23). The implication is that believing makes things possible. The question was not whether Jesus was able to heal the youth. The question was whether the man believed Jesus had to the ability to perform the task.

Upon hearing Jesus' response, the father cried out with tears, "*I do believe; help me overcome my unbelief!*" (Mark 9:24 NIV). The statement seems to be a clear contradiction at first blush. This man claimed he believed but in the same breath asked Jesus to help him with his lack of belief. The statement only made sense when I studied it in the original Greek. The word that was translated "unbelief" is actually the Greek word *apistia,* which means unfaithfulness or weakness of faith. A more telling translation of his plea would be "Lord, I believe in You, help my lack of faith."

Recall that Jesus had begun by chastising those present for their lack of faith; He referred to them as a faithless people. Subsequently, the man realized that his shortcoming was his lack of faith. This man already had hope, and he demonstrated belief when he came to the disciples because he heard and accepted that they had the power to cast out evil spirits. But by the time he got to Jesus he began to question whether a miracle could actually happen for his son. However, he understood Jesus' chastisement and wisely asked for help, given his lack of faith.

This man's story is one of my favorite anecdotes from the Bible because I can identify with his private struggle regarding faith. His inner turmoil belied a struggle between two realities—his current reality and a better future reality offered by Christ. He believed his son could be made well, and at the same time felt helpless over his son's condition. I've experienced similar struggles—one hand holding firm to a future reality promised by God and the other holding firm to a current reality filled with doubt and fear. In times past I have felt undeserving of God's promises because of my doubts. As a result, I failed to act on my beliefs. The revelation of the man's plea changed my life forever. I too began to pray, Lord, help my lack of faith.

The Word of God lets us know that we will encounter tests. Peter exhorts believers not to be surprised when we experience difficult trials because they reveal the glory of Christ that is in us (see 1 Pet. 4:12). This passage reminds us that our faith will be tested, and at times it will be difficult. When our faith is tested, we are at a point where two worlds collide; the present and future realities converge in our mind. If we accept the future reality that is promised by God, it overwhelms our current circumstances. Belief introduces options that before seemed improbable. That is why Jesus assured the boy's father that anything he believed was possible.

A SIGN OF BELIEF

By this time, the crowd of onlookers had grown as people began to flock to the scene. When Jesus observed this large crowd gathering, He demonstrated the power of the Kingdom of God. He commanded the deaf and mute spirit to come out of the youth and never enter him again. The subtleties of the account are remarkable. Although Jesus was simply informed of a spirit that had robbed the youth of his speech, He commanded the deaf and mute spirit to come out of him. Jesus knew precisely what He was dealing with and was able to directly address the boy's condition, commanding the spirit to leave permanently. Jesus did not offer temporary relief; instead, He provided a permanent cure.

The unclean spirit once again convulsed the boy violently and shrieked aloud. Nevertheless, at the command of Jesus, the spirit departed. In the aftermath, the youth lay motionless and seemingly lifeless, so much so that many onlookers assumed he was dead. Jesus, undeterred by the onlookers, took him by the hand and lifted him to his feet. This act is an important part of the story. Jesus was asked to cast out the unclean spirit. In other words, the request was for deliverance. However, Jesus offers much more when we place our trust in Him. He not only delivered the youth from the unclean spirit, but He ensured that he was fully recovered. He didn't leave him there lifeless; rather, He left him standing tall and full of life.

It is also important to note that Jesus performed this miracle in the presence of a sizeable crowd. Jesus taught His disciples that signs or miracles were largely for unbelievers' benefit. By this He meant that miracles were an opportunity for unbelievers to witness the power of God. The objective was not to cause unbelievers to seek miracles; rather, it was to cause them to accept the Word of God. Jesus had triumphed where His disciples had failed. In doing so He reaffirmed the truth in God's Word that mankind has authority in the earth. The father's belief in the words of Christ not only led to the deliverance of his son but was a source of encouragement to many others.

THESE SIGNS WILL FOLLOW YOU

The account of Jesus healing the boy with the evil spirit is just one of a number of miraculous accounts in the Gospel of Mark, and this Book concludes with an important passage of Scripture. True to His word, Jesus had overcome death, hell, and the grave. His death made salvation possible for all men, and His resurrection ushered in the Church age. He then spent a brief period of time following His resurrection imparting final teachings to those who would carry on His earthly ministry.

After instructing His disciples to carry the good news of the Kingdom to unbelievers in the 16th and final chapter of Mark, Jesus gave a final exhortation. He told His disciples that signs or miracles would accompany all who believe in Him. He gave several poignant examples, such as casting out evil spirits, speaking in foreign tongues, and healing sick people. Jesus had already demonstrated many of the miracles that He spoke of. His words assured them that they too were capable of miracles if they believed in Him.

Jesus' promise to the disciples extends to you and me today. God acts on our behalf when we believe in His faithfulness to perform His word. The primary reason Jesus performed miracles was to demonstrate the power we have access to as citizens of the Kingdom of God. Belief paves the way for God to transform our lives from the ordinary to the extraordinary. Belief makes us aware of the presence of God, and it is in the presence of God that we come to know Him and trust Him. And it is through knowledge of His Word that we have confidence that miraculous things are possible if we believe.

Chapter 3

Caught in the Act!

And without faith it is impossible to please God, because anyone who comes to Him must believe that He exists and that He rewards those who earnestly seek Him (Hebrews 11:6 NIV).

Few passages of Scripture resound in the heart of the believer the way the preceding verse does. The writer states rightly that faith is essential to pleasing God. In fact, the very premise of the verse is that the believer has a desire to please God. Recall that faith refers to our reliance on the words and intent of God. God is pleased when we place our trust in Him. In doing so, we acknowledge His role as Father and source. It is through the exercise of faith that we strengthen our relationship with Him. Thus, faith is the cornerstone of our relationship with God.

If we fail to exercise faith, we are unable to lead a life that pleases God. This may seem like a strong statement, but we must understand the nature of God. We are God's most prized creation—the only creatures designed to bear His image and share His nature. God is pleased when we display His character and abide by His Word. What's more, God is glorified when we act in faith. Faith enables the power and will of God to be manifested in the visible world. When this happens, God is glorified and His glory is spread throughout the earth.

This passage also gives a prescription for building our relationship with God. We note that anyone who seeks God must have confidence that God is real. Many people acknowledge that there is a higher power, and most refer to God by one name or another. However, they don't reverence Him as Lord of all living things. He is simply the God of their understanding. To many, God is a mysterious being they refer to instead of a personal Savior whom they can relate to. Acknowledging a personal God brings with it the responsibility of knowing Him and serving Him.

The last part of the verse should encourage anyone who desires to build a relationship with God. God rewards those who diligently seek Him. The true reward is not what many may initially think. This reward is not exemplified in material things, although those who serve God have access to such things. The true reward is the presence and influence of God in our lives. The Bible is very clear on this point. Men and women who demonstrate faith in God are favored by God. By that, I mean that God acts on their behalf. We note first and foremost that God establishes a relationship with men and women of faith, unlike others around them, and God speaks to them concerning their lives. God also gets involved in the situations that impact their lives. It is only when God gets involved in our lives that we know that He is truly real.

A SECOND OPINION

When she heard about Jesus, she came up behind Him in the crowd and touched His cloak, because she thought, "If I just touch His clothes, I will be healed" (Mark 5:27-28 NIV).

One of the most inspiring testimonies of faith occurred during an account of one of Jesus' many visits to Galilee. The story involves a woman who had suffered from a flow of blood for 12 years. Although the woman is not identified by name, the Bible gives us some insight into her life. The woman had been treated by many physicians and expended all her money in the process. But despite what was likely a sizable investment in medical treatment, her condition worsened. It is interesting to note that her health deteriorated under the care of supposed physicians, which demonstrates that human intellect alone is often insufficient.

It is also important to understand the physical nature and social implications of her illness. The flow of blood that she suffered from was a constant bleeding outside of a woman's normal cycle. According to Jewish law she was considered ceremonially unclean. This meant that she was not permitted to participate in temple worship. Those who were particularly pious may not have allowed her to come in contact with them because that too was prohibited by law. As such, her condition was both physically and emotionally debilitating.

Her account is actually a subplot of another story. Jesus had returned to Capernaum from one of His many ministry trips and was met by a large crowd who was anxiously awaiting His arrival. A synagogue ruler named Jairus made his way to Jesus and fell at His feet and worshipped Him. He then begged Jesus to come to his house to heal his 12-year-old daughter who was terminally ill. The girl was Jairus' only child, and he was deeply distressed because of her condition; yet he expressed his faith in Jesus. He declared that if Jesus would touch his daughter, she would get well and live.

Jesus, being moved by Jairus' plea and his expression of faith, readily agreed to go with him to heal his daughter. As they proceeded to his house, the crowd who followed Jesus continued to grow. Those who followed were no doubt interested to see what Jesus would do when He reached the house. The Bible notes that the crowd following Jesus pressed around Him so closely that they nearly crushed Him, and among this large crowd of people was the woman who suffered from the flow of blood.

The Bible provides limited details regarding the woman, and her identity is largely a mystery. In essence, the woman could be any one of us. Physicians may or may not have given up on her, but even so, her money had run out. She had endured the dreadful condition for what probably seemed like an eternity; this physical infirmity had become her mountain. Yet, while it seemed there was no cure for her condition, it just so happened that a renowned physician with revolutionary techniques was practicing in the region. So, she decided she would seek a second opinion from Him.

THE CONTINGENCY PLAN

Jesus' teachings and miracles were widely published across the region by this time, which is probably how the woman came to hear of Him. No doubt she'd heard accounts that He'd cast out devils and healed all manner of sickness, and what she heard concerning Jesus gave her hope for a cure. These accounts not only instilled hope but eventually led to her act of faith.

I wonder about her original plan. Most people generally conceive a plan when they want God to act on their behalf. Maybe she thought that she'd be one of the first to meet Him upon His return. Maybe she thought He would call her out of the crowd and lay hands on her. Whatever her original plan, we know the reality she actually encountered. When she arrived, she found Jesus thronged by a large crowd of people who were also anxiously awaiting His return to Galilee.

Would she be able to carry out her plan amidst these circumstances? In all likelihood, it didn't appear she would speak to Jesus at all. Many people often give up when God does not act according to their plan or schedule, but our heroine did not. When faced with adversity, she simply persevered. She decided in her mind that if she could just get close enough to touch His garment, she would receive her healing. Her thought process exemplified the very essence of belief. Her act of faith was bound to follow.

It would have been easy for this woman to have simply given up and accepted her condition. The size of the crowd and the intense press were difficult obstacles to overcome. Would it end in disappointment like her previous plans had? Can you see yourself in her experience? Maybe you have struggled with a physical or spiritual infirmity. Maybe you have repeatedly failed to achieve an important goal. Maybe you have a vision that others are reluctant to embrace. Maybe your dreams have come crashing down around you and you are struggling to rebuild them. The Bible records this woman's testimony in order to strengthen your faith.

Despite years of disappointment and numerous failed prescriptions, the heroine of our story kept searching for a cure. She believed in her heart that she would find it. Belief is the key to persistence. Have you encountered a situation that pushed you to the end of your natural ability? Have you ever wanted to achieve something that others believed impossible? Have you ever felt like there were obstacles in your life that were preventing you from being all that God purposed you to be? Maybe you feel that way right now. Just remember that God has the final word.

A Personal Touch

This woman fought her way through the crowd and touched the border of Jesus' garment as she had purposed in her heart. And once she touched His garment, she immediately knew she was healed. Her belief altered her reality, and she literally felt the Spirit of God move upon her. It is important to note that the Spirit moved as a direct result of her act of faith. In difficult times we are often our own biggest obstacle. We rely on our ability or intellect when we need to exercise faith. An act of faith says to God that we are willing and ready to place our welfare in His hands. Faith gives God the green light to change our condition.

After the woman was healed, Jesus asked who touched Him. The disciples thought it was an odd question because they all were being jostled about by the crowd, and Peter, speaking for the group, pointed out that all manner of people were pressing against Him. However, Peter did not understand the nature of the question. Jesus was not referring to a physical touch but a spiritual one. Jesus was keenly aware that the Spirit had moved and that power had been released. After all, that's what faith does. It releases power! Jesus then sought to identify the source of the faith that caused the Spirit to move.

Jesus could have continued on His way without saying a word. And if He had, this tremendous act of faith would have gone unrecognized. But He wanted to acknowledge the woman's act of faith for those present—and for generations to come. Jesus never missed an opportunity to demonstrate the power resident in the Kingdom of God. He also wanted to personally confirm what the woman sensed in her heart—that she had indeed been cured. We must understand that the exercise of faith is personal. Our personal relationship with God is the conduit for change in our lives.

The woman was surprised that her actions had been noticed and was quite nervous when she presented herself trembling at Jesus' feet. She then told Him of her illness and admitted what she had purposed in her heart. She proclaimed to Him and all present that when she had touched Him, she had instantly been healed. Upon hearing her spoken testimony, Jesus confirmed her miraculous healing. Moreover, He declared that her act of faith not only resulted in her physical healing, but it made her whole. The obstacle that had impaired her spiritual view had been cast away. The mountain that had impeded her progress in life had been removed. She was healthy both physically and spiritually, and all of it was a result of acting in faith.

Delayed but Not Denied

As you might imagine, this story has an interesting ending. While Jesus was yet speaking to the woman, a member of Jairus' household arrived bearing dreadful news. Recall that our story began with Jesus agreeing to attend to the daughter of Jairus, the synagogue ruler. On their journey towards his house, Jairus was informed that his daughter had died; hence, there was no need to bother Jesus any longer. What were Jairus' immediate thoughts? Maybe he was disappointed that Jesus had stopped to address the sick woman. Maybe he was angry with himself for not staying by his daughter's side. Whatever the case, he assuredly was overcome by grief and despair.

The news that Jairus received would have surely devastated him save one vital fact—he happened to be standing next to Jesus. There is an important principle to be observed. In life we will experience heartache and pain. Our relationship with God does not allow us to avoid heartache; it simply sustains us when we experience it. Therefore, like Jairus, we must stay close to Jesus. By definition, trying times are generally unexpected. Nevertheless, it is during trying times that we need to hear the Word of God most clearly.

Jesus overheard the report given to Jairus and countered with His own prognosis. Jairus had specifically requested that Jesus revive his daughter, and Jesus had every intention of honoring his request. Jesus promised Jairus that if he believed and did not doubt, his daughter would be healed. In essence, He told Jairus to keep believing. Jairus could not allow the negative report to extinguish his belief. He had to sustain the same level of faith he'd expressed when initially making his request. Jairus would soon find that his daughter's healing was simply delayed but not denied.

When Jesus arrived and found the family and friends mourning the girl's apparent death, He stated that the girl was not dead but asleep. Many of those present ridiculed Him because they felt certain the girl was dead. Undeterred, Jesus went into the house with a chosen few, including the parents and Peter, John, and James. Then Jesus took the girl by the hand and told her to get up. Just as He'd promised, the girl arose fully recovered.

Think about the subjects of our story and notice that their stories are distinct yet intertwined. We have the woman with the flow of blood who had suffered for 12 long years. We have the young girl with the terminal illness who had lived for only 12 short years. Both lives were fully restored because of the power released through faith. In the case of the woman with the flow of blood, there appeared to be no cure. In the case of the young girl, the cure appeared to arrive too late. We learn that when we place our trust in God, our blessing may be delayed but never denied.

We learn a great deal about faith through these miraculous account. We learn that God desires to be involved in our earthly affairs yet requires our faith to intervene. We learn that no matter how desperate a situation appears, God has the final word. We learn that if we add patience to our faith, God will honor our perseverance. Finally, we see the awesome possibilities as a result of the exercise of faith. Faith in God allows us to revive situations that otherwise seem hopeless.

PART II
TAKING INVENTORY

Taking Inventory

Examine me, O Lord, and try me; test my mind and my heart
(Psalm 26:2 NASB).

As I've matured in my walk with God, I've learned the vital
necessity of self-examination. I've also learned that this can only be
effectively accomplished through the power of God's Spirit. The
Bible ensures us that God faithfully rewards those who earnestly
seek Him. However, the Bible also tells us that we must seek God
with a pure heart. This speaks expressly to our desires. Faith is not
so much about what God does; rather, it is about who God is. The
manner and consistency with which we apply God's Word reveal
how well we know Him. Many people have difficulty exercising
faith because they don't have a personal relationship with God.
Faith is predicated on a strong relationship with God. In fact, it is a
natural by-product of the relationship. My pastor is fond of saying
that it is difficult to trust someone you do not know. It's his way of
admonishing the congregation to continually seek the presence of

God. God will never fail you. If you have difficulty trusting God, you need only to ask Him to search your heart.

The heart is the seat of our desires, inclinations, and emotions. It greatly influences our mind or the way we think. The Bible says that the human heart is more deceitful than anything else. It asks who can understand it (see Jer. 17:9). Your heart can betray you with respect to God's Word and His will if you do not allow God to examine you. God created you and only He can fully discern your true motives and reasoning. God knows your thoughts and your heart, and He will search you and test you, so that you realize your true motives and reasoning, and subsequently grow stronger in your faith. This is why the Bible tells us that God chastises His children whom He loves. He orchestrates the circumstances in our lives in such a way that His truths and our character are revealed.

The failure to examine one's heart gives place to thoughts, desires, or attitudes that are outside the will of God. This is not always a blatant violation. Most people who have driven an automobile are familiar with what is referred to as your blind spot. It's the location just over your left shoulder that is nearly impossible to see despite the aid of several peripheral devices installed in your vehicle. Whenever you are driving, your blind spot is there. Checking your blind spot before changing lanes is one of the most fundamental rules of defensive driving and is accomplished by completely turning your head to get a clear view. Once you check for danger, you can focus again on the road ahead. However, failure to check your blind spot puts both you and others in danger. Conversely, your observance of this fundamental rule keeps you out of harm's way and ensures that you arrive safely at your destination.

Our journey by faith is similar to taking a ride in an automobile. Although God leads us to our ultimate destination, we have what I refer to as spiritual blind spots. These include memories, emotions, desires, and inclinations that we store in our heart. As part of our subconscious, they go largely unaddressed or even unnoticed. Nonetheless, they greatly impact the way we view the world and are the basis for many of our decisions. What is most concerning about these elements of our inner man is that they alter or compromise our view of other people and the world around us. More importantly, they alter our understanding of God's Word, and without the proper understanding, we don't know how to entreat God. Yet this understanding only comes when we have the right perspective. For example, you won't ask for directions if you're unaware that you're lost. You won't ask for healing if you don't know you're wounded. And you won't ask for forgiveness if you're not aware that you've sinned. No matter how much knowledge we attain we must have the ability to view the world from God's perspective.

The wonderful thing about building a relationship with God is that He enables you to discover the real you. It should make sense. He is your Father, and you are made in His image and likeness. Christ is our example because He is the express image of God. He became a man so that you could get a good look at yourself. The key to navigating by faith is relatively straightforward: We must allow God to change our perspective. This is what David understood. He told God to examine him, testing his heart and mind, revealing any blind spots and more importantly revealing his true nature. We must likewise trust the Spirit and the Word of God to thoroughly search us. When I allowed God to search and test me, it revealed my blind spots as it related to the exercise of faith. I thank God for the light of His Word that reveals the hidden things of the heart. I also thank Him for chastising those whom He loves. His Word and His permissive will are working together to strengthen my faith. I pray that this section of the book will aid you in allowing God to examine your heart and build your faith.

CHAPTER 4

WHAT ARE YOU HOPING FOR?

May the God of hope fill you with all joy and peace as you trust in Him, so that you may overflow with hope by the power of the Holy Spirit (Romans 15:13 NIV).

What's your motivation? What gets you out of bed in the morning? What are you hoping for? This may sound strange, but I would argue that it is the life that you expect to live. You may be content or even delighted with your present circumstances, but by design you are hardwired to think that life can and will get better. That's what hope is all about—a desire for a future reality that is both favorable and possible.

Recall from Chapter 1 that we highlighted Paul's letter to the assembly at Rome. Hope was a recurring theme throughout his letter where he spoke of joy and peace that comes only as a result of hope in God. Paul closes the body of the letter by entreating God to fill his fellow believers with an abundance of hope through the Holy Spirit—not hope in temporal things but rather hope in the eternal Kingdom of God. I like to refer to this as *heavenly hope*.

What is *heavenly hope*? If hope is closely tied to our desires, then it follows that *heavenly hope* is founded upon our relationship with God. Said another way, heavenly hope is inspired by the Word of God.

filled with victorious testimonies from the lives of
—testimonies that ignite hope in the hearts of read-
ame way, your personal testimony provides encour-
ation for others.

It is vital that our hope is in the Word of God. As Paul rightly asserts, this type of hope comes only through the inner working of the Holy Spirit. Hope placed in anything other than God's Word is not sure. When our desires are in agreement with the Word of God, we have assurance of what we hope for. It is only when our desires agree with the Word of God that He gives us the desires of our heart.

Heavenly hope has three distinguishing characteristics that we will examine in this chapter. First, we understand that heavenly hope has an eternal focus. God's destiny for your life is more important than your present circumstances. Second, we see that heavenly hope leads to endless possibilities. It is a gift from God that enables you to continue during tough times. Finally, hope makes life worth living. Hope is fire that fuels the dreams that God places in your heart. Let's examine the life-sustaining power of hope.

BLESSED ASSURANCE

For my eyes have seen Your salvation, which You have prepared in the sight of all people, a light for revelation to the Gentiles and for glory to Your people Israel (Luke 2:30-32 NIV).

The second chapter of Luke records the account of Jesus' dedication to the Lord. Mosaic law required that a firstborn son be consecrated or set apart for service to the Lord. While this event had a literal meaning during the time of Moses, it was more of a figurative gesture during Jesus' day. The practice involved presenting the child to the priest at the temple in Jerusalem. It was also customary for a family to offer a sacrifice for the mother, signaling her purification following childbirth. Joseph and Mary made the five-mile trip from Bethlehem to Jerusalem to consecrate their firstborn son as well as to offer the sacrifice for Mary.

Meanwhile, there was a man in Jerusalem by the name of Simeon. He is believed to have been an older man and is described as just and devout. The Bible also informs us that the Spirit of the Lord was upon him. His heart's greatest desire was to see the Lord's Christ, who would deliver Israel. While the story of Simeon is not a popularized account, it is one of the clearest examples of *heavenly hope*. Simeon's hope was not motivated by personal gain but by a righteous desire to witness God's will manifested in the earth. Unbeknownst to Joseph and Mary, the baby Jesus had a divine appointment with a faithful servant.

In order to appreciate Simeon's story, we have to consider the conditions of the time. The Roman Empire was the dominant power of the day, ruling many nations, including the remnant of the nation of Israel. In Israel, the prophets of old had prophesied of a Messiah who would sit on the throne of David and who would be the Savior of their people. The greatest hope among Jews was the arrival of the Lord's Christ, or Anointed One. This Anointed One would not only deliver Israel, but restore the nation to a position of prominence. The dominance of the Romans further fueled the hopes of Jews for the arrival of the Anointed One.

Simeon, like most devout Jews, was well acquainted with the books of the law and related prophecies. However, there was something more at work in his life. Simeon had a close relationship with God exemplified by the fact that the Holy Spirit rested on his life. We learn that the Holy Spirit revealed to Simeon that he would not die until he had seen the Anointed One, and that promise became his source of inspiration. He had comfort in knowing that God had assured him of his heart's greatest desire.

We often associate the blessings or favor of God with material things, and if we are not careful, we may treat God as if He is a genie in a bottle. It is important that we understand the vital necessity of building a meaningful relationship with God and the true benefit derived from this relationship—this most significant benefit being that He speaks to us concerning our lives. His favor is demonstrated by His willingness to give us clarity and direction. Simeon was at peace because he had heard from God. Therefore, he had confidence that he would not die until his hope was realized.

Most people today have difficulty accepting the notion that the God of the universe will speak directly to them. That's right! The God of all creation desires to commune with you. Genesis records that God visited the Garden of Eden regularly to speak with Adam. Communication is the basis for any strong relationship. In one of his many Psalms, David marvels at the high regard God has for man (see Ps. 8:4). Our lives are full of hope when we accept that God stands ready and willing to speak to us concerning His plan for our lives.

MY EYES HAVE SEEN THE GLORY

When Joseph and Mary arrived at the temple with their infant son, Simeon was in the temple courts waiting to meet them. It's clear that Simeon had established a relationship with God, and as the Bible declares, God rewards those who diligently seek Him. The Holy Spirit not only led him to the temple that day but identified the child Jesus upon His arrival. Overcome with joy, Simeon swept the child into his arms and began to glorify God. He had patiently waited for that which he'd hoped. Moreover, Simeon believed God's promise, and thus his heart was open to receive instruction from the Holy Spirit.

With Jesus lying in his arms, Simeon began to prophesy concerning Him. Simeon not only pronounced Him Savior of Israel, but he was the first person in the Gospels to declare Jesus' ministry to the Gentile world. In essence, Simeon acknowledged Jesus as Savior and King of all mankind. Through the revelation of the Holy Spirit, Simeon declared God's sovereign plan for all nations.

Simeon also prepared Mary for the difficulty she would endure. While the Bible is silent as to the exact timing and nature of Joseph's death, we know that he is not on the scene during the time of Jesus' ministry and subsequent crucifixion. Simeon informed Mary that while Jesus would uplift and encourage many, He would also cause the fall of those who do not truly serve God. He would be spoken against and persecuted. Simeon warned Mary that these things would affect her greatly because of her love for her son. God often prepares us for the difficult times that lie ahead.

Simeon then made an incredible statement at this point in the story. He declared that he was now ready to depart from his present life having seen the Messiah. Following this account, we don't read anymore of Simeon. It is likely that he passed away shortly thereafter. Simeon probably never witnessed a miracle, he likely never heard Jesus teach, and he was not present when Jesus died on the cross; yet he was satisfied having been in the presence of Jesus Christ. He was content knowing that God's plan was being manifested in the earth. What an amazing testimony. His story teaches us to place our hope in God and not simply to desire the things He can provide.

KEEPING HOPE ALIVE

Like many biblical accounts, this story has an interesting conclusion. While Simeon was prophesying regarding the child Jesus, another person was listening nearby. Anna, a prophetess and a descendant of the tribe of Asher, had been coming to the temple every day to worship. This elderly widow, whose husband had passed shortly after their marriage, could always be found in the temple faithfully fasting and praying. In fact, the Bible tells us that she followed this routine daily. Hearing Simeon, she gave thanks to God for the arrival of the Messiah. She then departed, sharing the good news with others who were looking toward the coming of the Messiah.

Anna, like Simeon, was a faithful servant of God, which is demonstrated in her commitment to worship and prayer. While the Bible does not tell us that she had an explicit promise from God, she was blessed just the same. Her faithfulness over the years was rewarded by her meeting with the Messiah. She certainly could have been disillusioned by the death of her husband; but instead, she turned her focus to the things of God. Again, we see that hope in God never fails.

Simeon and Anna are lasting examples of individuals who embodied *heavenly hope*. Figuratively and literally, their hope kept them alive.

Heavenly hope gives life meaning. With the Word of God as our focus, our lives are full of peace and joy. That is what Simeon and Anna experienced—the peace of knowing that God's Spirit was leading them and the joy of knowing that God rewards faithfulness.

A LIFE WORTHY OF LIVING

At the beginning of this chapter, we discussed that *heavenly hope* has an eternal focus. Temporal things are never the focus of *heavenly hope* because possessions come and go. This is why the Bible tells us to set our affection on things above (see Col. 3:2). In a practical sense, this implies that we should share the same desires as God the Father. When we desire to do the will of God, He carefully involves us in His plan for mankind. Our hope does not disappoint because we see the will of God manifested in our daily lives.

An eternal focus also means that we do not allow temporal circumstances to diminish our hope. In difficult times it is easy to lose hope. At these times, we often shift our focus from eternal things to temporal things. Career, finances, broken relationships, and countless other distractions can take our focus away from God. I've learned that my career, finances, and even family and friends at times may fail. But God never fails. That is why my hope is centered on His Word.

Heavenly hope is about possibilities rather than probabilities. During our lives we become conditioned to think in terms of probabilities or likely outcomes. We base our decisions on our experience or the experiences of others. While we can certainly learn from our experiences, we must be careful not to place limitations on God. God has a knack for doing things that by our way of thinking are improbable. That is why the Bible affirms that with God all things are possible (see Mark 10:27). God by His very nature offers endless possibilities.

Heavenly hope blows probability out of the water. It inspires people to think outside the box and dismiss conventional wisdom. This hope leads to innovative discoveries and superior outcomes because people are motivated to try new things. Individuals with *heavenly hope* are not content with the status quo; instead, they blaze new trails despite the odds.

Finally, *heavenly hope* makes life worth living because it causes us to usher the unseen into the seen world. I like to say that hope is the stuff that dreams are made of. This is because hope is what drives you until your dreams become a reality. When you are full of hope, your dreams never die. *Heavenly hope* makes life worth living because God is the source of your heart's earnest desires and lifelong dreams. Rejoice in the hope of the glory of God.

CHAPTER 5

ARE YOU READY TO RECEIVE?

But the good soil represents those who hear and accept God's message and produce a huge harvest—thirty, sixty or even a hundred times as much as had been planted (Mark 4:20 NLT).

Jesus often taught in parables, and one of the most familiar parables from the Bible is commonly referred to as the parable of the sower. In this parable, a farmer went out to sow seed, and the scattered seed fell in different places. Some seed fell beside the road, some on rocky ground, some among thorns, and some on fertile soil. While most of the seed failed to yield fruit because of the condition of the ground, the fertile soil proved to be the exception, producing a large crop.

In His explanation to the disciples, Jesus highlighted the essential nature of the parable, suggesting that if they understood this parable, it would give them insight into all the other parables. I've heard many expositions of this parable, but I believe the ground is a metaphor for the human heart and the seed represents God's Word. The condition of our heart determines whether we accept and obey God's Word. This is vitally important because the quality of our lives is inextricably linked to our faith in God's Word.

Let's further examine the different types of ground. The wayside was a road or footpath for walking. It was a well-trodden ground not able to receive seed, and so, the birds quickly came and took the seed away. The rocky ground was a place of shallow soil with rock underneath. Without cultivation to loosen this soil and remove the rocks, the roots could not take hold in this ground, and the plant would die before yielding fruit. The thorny ground was also incapable of producing crops. Beneath the thick and thistle was soil appropriate for growing crops, but the thorns prevented them from flourishing.

Then there was the fertile ground that produced in abundance. This fertile ground was the only type of ground that was prepared to receive seed—and the operative word here is *prepared*. I like to view *prepared* as work done in advance. When we think about faith, we often think of the supernatural, but think about this simple example Jesus used. The economy in the region of Palestine where Jesus ministered was dominated by agriculture. Consequently, most of His listeners could easily relate to a parable about sowing seed. The parable begins at the point of sowing seed, but anyone familiar with farming knows that the ground must first be prepared to receive seed. Tough soil must be broken up and large rocks removed. Thorns and thistle must also be taken away. In much the same way, we must prepare ourselves— our hearts—to receive God's Word.

A great teacher once made a profound statement that I will never forget. He noted that preparation is the surest demonstration of what a person believes. If you believe you will pass an exam, then you prepare for it; and in your preparation, you don't expect to fail. Likewise, if you believe God's Word, you prepare for what He promises. The fact that you are reading this book is evidence that you believe God can and will do great things in your life. What great thing has God promised you that you have yet to prepare for? What's preventing you from getting ready?

LET DOWN YOUR NETS

And He entered into one of the ships, which was Simon's, and prayed him that he would thrust out a little from the land. And He sat down, and taught the people out of the ship. Now when He had left speaking, He said unto Simon, Launch out into the deep, and let down your nets for a draught (Luke 5:3-4 KJV).

Many of the principles we learn through the Scriptures are derived from the lessons that Jesus taught His disciples. One of the most essential lessons was conveyed to His inner circle of disciples at the very beginning of their time with Jesus. The brothers Simon and Andrew and the brothers James and John were commercial fishermen by trade, and the Sea of Galilee in northern Palestine served as the base for their business. This region was a center for commercial fishing as well as a thriving marketplace during Jesus' day.

It was customary for fishermen to take their boats out overnight while the water was cool and the fish ventured closer to the surface. They would move out into the deeper waters and let their nets down for a catch. During the day, they would engage in various other tasks, including selling fresh fish at market, preserving fish to be shipped, purchasing supplies, and mending nets. While a thriving fishing business might produce handsome profits, it required strenuous, messy work.

Shortly after beginning His public ministry, Jesus traveled throughout Palestine preaching good news concerning the Kingdom of Heaven; and wherever He went, He was thronged by crowds of people. One day, as Jesus was preaching on the shore of the Sea of Galilee, a large crowd gathered, pressing in on Him as He spoke. Noticing two empty fishing boats nearby, Jesus approached Simon, the owner of one of the boats, and asked Simon to push off a little from shore so that He could speak to the crowd from the boat. Simon acquiesced, allowing Jesus to finish His address from the boat.

After He'd finished preaching, Jesus instructed Simon to go out into the deep water and let down his nets for a large catch—an odd request given it was the middle of the day. Recall that it was customary for fishermen to fish overnight. What's more, Simon informed Jesus that the crew had toiled the previous night and hadn't caught anything. It's safe to say that Simon didn't feel much like fishing at that time. Nevertheless, Simon told Jesus that he would make another attempt because of His instruction.

Simon's reply suggests that he was complicit with Jesus' instruction. However, I believe his words belied the cynicism that we see demonstrated by Simon in various other accounts found in the Scriptures. Simon wanted it understood that he was following this questionable course of action only at Jesus' behest. He did not expect to catch any fish and was hardly interested in wasting time on what he undoubtedly thought was a fruitless endeavor.

CATCH OF THE DAY

It's easy to pick on Simon. After all, he's not around to defend himself. However, we must examine our own actions in response to God's Word. There have been times when I've personally doubted the promises tied to the instructions I've received from God's Word. This doubting then led to uncertain efforts and uncertain results. In the case of Simon, Jesus did not simply instruct him to let down his nets; Jesus told Simon to let down his nets for a draught, or a large catch. The promise of an abundant catch was implicit in the instructions. While God's promises are sure, we must be qualified to receive them. First and foremost, we must obey God's instructions. Obedience is synonymous with faith. Moreover, we must be ready to receive. It's sort of like expecting an important delivery. You have to make arrangements to receive the thing that is promised in order to enjoy the benefits.

When Simon's crew pushed out into the deep, they were hardly prepared for what would happen next. They began to catch more fish than their nets could contain. In fact, the Scriptures inform us that their nets began to break. One might rightly surmise that their nets merely gave way under the weight of the fish. Nevertheless, we must not miss the important lesson here. The crew neither expected nor prepared to catch a large number of fish. The condition of their nets was a metaphor for their lack of faith.

Realizing his crew was ill prepared for the large catch, Simon signaled to his partners in the other boat near shore. James and John were the owners of the second boat and Simon's partners in the fishing venture. The two boats worked together, hauling in so many fish that each boat began to sink. Jesus had a large blessing in store for Simon and his partners, yet Simon's unbelief nearly caused them to miss it. When the fishermen became overwhelmed by the large catch, Simon realized the error in his ways.

While Simon's offense may not have been obvious to those around, Simon was keenly aware of his shortcoming. He hadn't believed the promise of Jesus nor trusted His instructions, and his halfhearted actions were carried out simply to appease Jesus. He had not prepared for the large catch Jesus had promised, and in turn, he did not feel worthy of such a blessing. Afterward, he fell to his knees before Jesus, declaring himself to be a sinful man and asking Jesus to depart from him because of his unbelief. Like Simon, we must understand that unbelief is a weakness of the heart that must be overcome.

FISHING FOR MEN

Jesus was not put off by Simon's actions at all. If you haven't gathered by now, Jesus was about His business of fishing for men. Unbeknownst to Simon, he'd been selected to join Jesus in the expansion of a new enterprise. While Jesus had many disciples, Simon would be counted among the twelve who would become his closest companions. Simon had many admirable qualities, including boldness and tenacity. He was a vocal leader who influenced those around him. Jesus understood that Simon was not easily persuaded, so He orchestrated the situation to cause Simon and the other disciples to believe.

Many scholars and casual readers alike assume that this interaction was the first between Jesus and His recruits. I personally believe that the men were already acquainted with Jesus and his teachings. Jesus was purposeful in his actions and likely had already identified these men through real-life interactions. To recruit them for the work He intended, Jesus engaged them in their element, and He was masterful at identifying with His followers—what better way to recruit fishermen than to spend a day on the boat with them. What we refer to as the call of the disciples in all likelihood was the culmination of Jesus' recruitment effort.

Jesus concluded his efforts by offering the men the opportunity of a lifetime. Jesus told them if they joined Him, He would make them fishers of men. Simon, Andrew, James, and John were already experienced fishermen; however, what they witnessed that day contradicted their knowledge and experience with respect to fishing. They were fishing at the wrong time and with less than adequate provisions, yet they hauled in their largest catch ever. After such an amazing display of power, how could they refuse His offer?

Preparing the Way

Earlier in this book, we established that belief is a prerequisite for receiving the promises of God. It is our confidence in God's ability to perform His Word that opens the door for Him to intervene in our affairs. Conversely, doubt hinders God from working in our lives because He cannot go against our will. Doubt is a subtle yet dangerous intruder. Though it may creep in at times, we must drive it from our dwelling place. If we harbor doubt, we may find ourselves unprepared or unqualified to receive the promises of God. Doubt often rears its ugly head when we receive instructions from God. Doubt can paralyze you if you allow it, so you must be disciplined and make ready for the things that God promises.

Further examination of Jesus' interaction with His recruits reveals an interesting pattern that we see often in Scripture. It was after teaching the truths of God that Jesus called the recruits to action. Teaching prepares our hearts and minds to receive instructions from God. The Word of God is your only offensive weapon, and it arms you to do the will of God. Belief always precedes the exercise of faith. This is because we act only on what we believe. I'm fond of telling those whom I teach that my objective goes beyond conveying knowledge of the Scriptures; my ultimate objective is to persuade my listeners and readers to believe God's Word. The Bible admonishes us not to forsake assembling together as a body of believers (see Heb. 10:25), and one of the primary reasons we assemble is to be taught the Word of God.

While obedience is the key to realizing the promises of God, preparation is an essential first step. Preparation is both an internal and external activity. Internally, you must prepare your heart and mind. Your heart is your reservoir for storing God's Word. This is also the place where you store your meditations, desires, inclinations, and the like. The things you store in your heart determine how you view the world. In preparation for God's promises, you must rid your heart of anything that does not agree with His Word. This is not a one-time event, rather an ongoing pursuit. Your mind represents the way you think or, better stated, the way you make decisions. In order to make good (godly) decisions, you must replace your old decision criteria with the truth prescribed in God's Word.

Externally, you must engage in actions that demonstrate your readiness to receive. If you want to prosper financially, you must be a better steward of your current resources. This may require paying off debt, curbing spending habits, or regular tithing. If you want to grow spiritually, you must engage in activities that promote spiritual growth. These include worship, prayer, reading, and attending church meetings. James said it best when he declared that he demonstrated his faith by his works (see James 2:18). James was not referring to empty religious activities; he was speaking of his earnest demonstration of what he believed. God desires that we put His Word to the test. He admonishes us to try Him and see that He will shower us with more blessings than we can receive (see Mal. 3:10).

CHAPTER 6

WHAT DO YOU HAVE TO GIVE?

*Give, and it will be given to you. They will pour into your lap a
good measure—pressed down, shaken together and running over.
For by your standard of measure, it will be measured to you in
return* (Luke 6:38 NASB).

One evening Jesus went to a mountain and prayed through the night.
As He was at this time, Jesus could often be found in prayer prior to significant decisions or events. When morning arrived, He called together
His disciples, who at the time were many in number, and selected twelve
to be apostles, or special messengers. These twelve would be His inner
circle and His closest companions during the latter stages of His ministry. They would also be commissioned to continue His ministry after
His departure and would become the leaders of the early Church.

Immediately after His selection, He went down the mountainside
to a large crowd who had gathered. This crowd was made up of His
followers as well as a great number of people from far and near who
had come to hear Him preach and be healed of many sicknesses. Jesus
then delivered a pivotal message with valuable insight for anyone who
aspires to walk in faith. He addressed love, forgiveness, and generosity—three things that are required prior to enjoying God's promises.

While each of these is important in its own right, it is the act of giving that is essential to unlocking the riches of God's Kingdom.

Recall from Chapter 4 that God's Kingdom is eternal and material things are temporal; and we run into problems when we have a temporal focus. When material things become our focus, we cannot exercise faith. It's like saying to God that we do not trust Him to provide for us. This is why Jesus tells us to store up things in Heaven, because those things are eternal. When our desires become solely set on the things God provides and not God Himself, we lose our focus. This is why Jesus also instructs us to first seek the Kingdom. This means that the will of God must supercede our own desires. And when we make God's will our priority, He promises to reward our faithfulness.

The promises of God are exclusive rights that are conferred as a result of our relationship with Him. One such promise relates to giving. Jesus states plainly that if we give to others, we will receive from God. Notice that giving precedes receiving. When we are generous, we not only demonstrate our faith in God, but we display the nature of God. Giving is a requirement, and God fully expects us to be generous in our giving. We must give from a pure heart, requiring nothing in exchange. We must have faith that the same God who requires us to give will fulfill His promise to recompense our giving.

It is interesting to note that most people readily associate prosperity with faith. There is a very good reason for this. God desires that those who serve Him prosper both naturally and spiritually. The believer understands that Christ is Lord and ruler of all and that the mature believer is a joint heir with Christ. A key aspect of faith is reliance on God as our source for all things—natural and spiritual.

I am fully convinced that many people struggle in life because they have not embraced giving. They want God to bless them abundantly, yet they have not exhibited faith in God. People who are unwilling to give liberally of their time and substance do not trust God. They've wittingly or unwittingly adopted a carnal mentality that produces selfish behavior. Jesus clearly explains that God's ability to reward you is regulated by your willingness to give to others. Giving not only opens the faucet but increases the flow of blessings in your life. Blessings can either trickle out or pour out—it's up to you. There are some people who seem to prosper, yet fail to demonstrate generosity. Bear in mind, material things are temporal. The eternal riches of God are reserved for those who worship Him and are liberal in their giving.

GOD WANTS TO USE YOU

As evening approached, the disciples came to Him and said, "This is a remote place, and it's already getting late. Send the crowds away, so they can go to the villages and buy themselves some food." Jesus replied, "They do not need to go away. You give them something to eat" (Matthew 14:15-16 NIV).

While traveling near the Sea of Galilee, Jesus received word of the execution of John the Baptist. John, who had preached the message of repentance preparing the way for Jesus' ministry, was related to Jesus; he was the son of Elizabeth, the cousin of Jesus' mother. Jesus no doubt was affected by the news and departed privately to a remote place. Nevertheless, the crowds followed Him, bringing many people with various infirmities. Although Jesus likely desired some time to Himself, He had compassion on the multitude and healed all who were sick.

Since it was very late and they were in a remote place, the disciples suggested that Jesus send the crowd away so they could go to the near-by villages to purchase food. The disciples had been busy themselves and hadn't had anything to eat. They were now ready to see the crowd dispersed so they could tend to their own needs. Jesus seized this opportunity to teach them a valuable lesson concerning giving and faith. He told His disciples that there was no need for the crowd to depart and instructed them to give the crowd food to eat.

Imagine the perplexed look on the disciples' faces when they heard His response. As they looked out over the endless sea of faces, they discounted His instruction as an impossible request. After all, they didn't have any food themselves. Even if they'd had provisions, they would not have been able to accommodate such a large number of people. Moreover, they were tired at this point and the last thing on their minds was serving such a large group. Think of the irony—the disciples had been traveling with Jesus for some time and had seen Him perform countless miracles, yet they stumbled whenever He directed them to do something that was out of the ordinary.

The challenge the disciples encountered was no different than what you or I face today. Many people actually believe in miracles. We accept that Jesus walked on water, healed the sick, or even raised the dead. However, we struggle when it involves us personally. Because we don't truly know God and His will for our lives, we don't believe He will work through us to perform miracles. However, that is exactly what God wants to do. The Bible tells us that the eyes of the Lord go all about searching for people that He can empower (see 2 Chron. 16:9). In other words, God wants to do miraculous things through your life so that His glory is seen in the earth.

YOU HAVE A LOT TO OFFER

Jesus already knew that He would feed the multitude. His focus now turned to building His disciples' faith. He first questioned His disciple Philip and asked where they could buy bread to feed the large crowd. If we study Scripture, we observe that Philip was the concerned type. He liked to deal with facts and figures and could be somewhat pessimistic. Jesus knew that Philip had sized up the situation and was prepared with an informed reply. Philip told Jesus that eight months' wages would not be sufficient to provide even a small portion for such a large crowd. The implication was that they did not have enough money to consider such a course of action. Jesus was testing Philip. He wanted to make sure that what was about to happen would resonate with Philip and deeply affect his faith.

Undeterred by Philip's response, Jesus sent the disciples to find food among those gathered. Shortly thereafter, Andrew returned with a young boy who had five barley loaves and two fish.

Apparently this food was all that their search produced. Accordingly, the disciples remained doubtful, asking what use such small provisions were among such a large crowd. Jesus then ordered the disciples to bring the five loaves and the two small fish to Him.

Jesus' instruction to bring the provisions to Him is the pivotal point of the account. The disciples were failing because they had been relying on their own strength. However, God never gives us an assignment without supplying the provisions. Miracles take place when we are willing to act without a guarantee. Jesus was prepared to work a miracle, but He wanted to involve the disciples. By sending them to search for food, He was in essence asking them to offer what they had to give.

No matter the situation, you always have something to give. Maybe it is something material; maybe it is a sacrifice of time; maybe it is simply the sacrifice of praise or thanksgiving. Whatever the case, you always have something to give. If you want God to do something miraculous in your life, I have some unconventional advice: Look for an opportunity to give. Your generosity proves to God that you are qualified to receive His promises. An essential part of abundant living in the earth is discovering what it is you have to offer the world and then giving it as God's Spirit leads.

MORE THAN ENOUGH

After instructing the crowd to sit down, Jesus looked to the Father in Heaven, gave thanks, and blessed the provisions. He then gave the provisions to the disciples to distribute to the people. The Bible records that the entire crowd ate until they were full—a crowd who numbered 5,000 men, not accounting for the women and children. After everyone had eaten their fill, the disciples were instructed by Jesus to collect the leftovers so that nothing would be wasted. The disciples collected twelve baskets full of leftovers.

We are often like the disciples, limiting God's ability to work through us because we are unwilling to offer what we have to give. When Jesus instructed the disciples to feed the multitude, their response should have been to produce whatever it was they had to offer. This is because Jesus had already proven He was able to supernaturally increase whatever they had. Jesus did not need the disciples' contribution to feed the crowd; however, He wanted to teach them that if they trusted God, He would reward their faith.

Notice that Jesus began by giving thanks. The disciples were so concerned with what they didn't have that they did not thank God for what He'd already provided. Jesus understood that God can turn our little into a lot. He demonstrated that when you are in covenant with God, He is responsible for your well-being. When we fail to give thanks, we characterize God as a poor Father, calling into question His ability to provide for us. David admonishes believers to give praise, be thankful, and bless the name of God in order to enter His presence (see Ps. 100:4). When we show gratitude for the things God provides and dedicate them to Him, He responds by blessing and multiplying our provisions.

There was precedence for this type of occurrence long before the days of Jesus. During the days of Elisha the prophet, there was a famine in Palestine. One day, when a man brought Elisha a sack of grain and 20 small loaves of barley (see 2 Kings 4:42), Elisha commanded that they be given to a group of one hundred prophets to eat. The servant questioned Elisha, stating that one hundred men could not be fed with such small provisions. But Elisha simply repeated his command, adding that there would be plenty for all. Elisha was confident because he had received a promise from God. True to Elisha's words, the men were filled, and there was plenty left over. Elisha simply trusted God to fulfill His promise to provide for His people.

There is an important parallel between these two accounts. In both instances, there was an offering, which was followed by God's increase. The blessings of God will always follow your sacrifice if your motives are pure. Remember the promise cited early in this chapter. "Give and it will be given to you." This is a promise from God. Giving demonstrates your faith in God and, in turn, qualifies you to receive the promises of God. What's more, if you give liberally, you are promised blessings that overflow or exceed your expectations.

SECOND TIME AROUND

To say that feeding thousands of people with a meal offered by a young boy is miraculous is an understatement. One would think that this type of event would have had an immutable effect on the mentality of the disciples. However, we don't have to travel far in Scripture to observe the actual effect of this demonstration on the disciples. In the very next chapter of the Book of Matthew, Jesus is again ministering on a mountainside near Galilee (see Matt. 15:32). Large crowds had followed Him, and for three days they continued with Him. After Jesus healed the people of all their afflictions, they praised God and would not depart, despite going three days with little or no food.

Jesus then called His disciples to Him to speak with them concerning the people. He told the disciples that He did not want to send the people away hungry and was concerned that in this condition they might faint on their return to their respective homes. Bear in mind that a short time before, the disciples had witnessed Jesus feed over five thousand people with five barley loaves and two fish. Jesus once again was testing His disciples' faith.

Unlike the first occasion, the disciples actually had some small provisions with them this time. However, when Jesus told them of His intentions to feed the crowd, they immediately began to question Him and exclaimed that there was no way they could find enough bread in their remote location to feed such a large crowd (a crowd numbering four thousand men, not counting the women and children). Jesus asked them a simple but profound question. How many loaves do you have? Said another way—what do you have to give?

As it turned out, the disciples had seven loaves and a few small fish. Think carefully about the details of this account. The disciples had recently witnessed Jesus feed a larger crowd with fewer provisions, yet faced with the same circumstance, they did not act in faith. Nonetheless, just as before, Jesus took the food and gave thanks.

Following this, He gave it to the disciples and had them distribute it to the people. Again, the entire multitude ate until they were filled, and the disciples collected seven baskets of leftovers.

Don't Bury Your Treasure

Why didn't the disciples get it the first time? The same reason you and I don't always get it at first. To reiterate an earlier premise, knowledge does not equal belief. Even after having witnessed the miraculous works of Jesus, the disciples still often struggled with their faith. Likewise, we sometimes struggle despite our knowledge of God's Word. Faith grows as a result of responding to the Word of God. Faith does not work according to our experience; rather, it works in spite of our experience. Faith requires us to act on what we know and not what we see. In the disciples' case, faith meant to offer up whatever means they had to feed the people in spite of how small the provisions appeared.

Now the question is posed to you. What do you have to give? What resources has God furnished you with—material or otherwise—that you are holding back? What gifts, talents, or abilities do you have to offer the world that will glorify God and provide for your well-being? What praise and worship can you offer that will draw others to Christ and His Kingdom? What encouragement or godly counsel can you offer to benefit those around you? If you want to walk in faith, stop looking outside yourself and start looking within.

In his second letter to the assembly at Corinth, Paul speaks of a treasure contained in earthen vessels (see 2 Cor. 4:7). The treasure Paul refers to is the revelation of God's Word and the Gospel of His Kingdom. The phrase "earthen vessel" is translated from a Greek phrase that means clay pot. In ancient times, it was customary to bury treasures inside clay pots. God loves us so much that He has entrusted us with this priceless treasure, and He does this in spite of the fact that our human bodies are frail and fallible. The gift of the Holy Spirit enables us to preserve this wonderful treasure. God has richly endowed us so that we can be a blessing to those we come into contact with. The greatest gift that we can offer the world is the Gospel of Christ the King and His Kingdom. This treasure is freely given to us and, in turn, we must freely give it away. Spreading the Gospel message is the greatest responsibility of every believer. Our obedience to this charge demonstrates our love for God and our faith in His Word.

PART III
BUILDING TRUST

BUILDING TRUST

Do not worry then, saying, "What will we eat?" or "What will we drink?" or "What will we wear for clothing?" For the Gentiles eagerly seek all these things; for your heavenly Father knows that you need all these things. But seek first His Kingdom and His righteousness, and all these things will be added to you (Matthew 6:31-33 NASB).

This popular passage of Scripture is paramount to building trust in God. In these verses, Jesus admonishes His followers to seek the Kingdom of God and His righteousness. The Kingdom of God refers to God's rule through the human heart, and righteousness in this context refers to God's will. To seek God's Kingdom and righteousness means to allow God to rule your thoughts and actions and to make His will your primary concern. The Kingdom of God, while at present an invisible reality, will someday be manifested in the earth. God's original plan, and ultimate end, is for man to rule in the earth as He does in Heaven. This is how we bear the image and likeness of our Father.

Reading in context we find that Jesus chastised His followers concerning their level of faith and told them not to become preoccupied with the accumulation of material possessions. Therefore, it is important that we view our material possessions in the proper context. Material wealth is temporal and is not to be confused with the eternal riches of God's Kingdom. We should value giving to others above collecting material possessions for personal enjoyment. In this way, we ensure that we are rewarded in God's eternal Kingdom. We can easily become motivated by greed or covetousness if we are not careful. This is because the world generally associates financial prosperity with contentment. However, an intimate relationship with God is the only thing in life that offers true contentment. If money or property is our primary aim, we exhibit a lack of faith in God—the source of all natural and spiritual wealth.

Jesus often warned about the deceitful nature of riches. This refers to the misplaced trust that people place in material things. When hearing statements about these kind of people, we naturally think of people who have an abundance of money and possessions. However, misplaced trust is an equally dangerous tendency of those who have moderate or little material wealth. He cautioned those of modest means against needless worry about provisions such as food, drink, and clothes. When we worry about our perceived lack of material possessions or daily provisions, we exist in a perpetual state of insecurity. This constant concern robs us of our peace, joy, and countless other spiritual blessings that come from God. Stated another way, it robs us of our abundant life promised by Christ Jesus.

People commonly worry about material needs, because they fail to seek assurance aside from themselves. When we come to know the character of God and His love for us, we understand that we needn't worry about material things. God knows that we have natural needs, and He is able and willing to supply our needs. He simply desires that we establish the proper priority. Jesus gives us the key when He tells us to seek the Kingdom of God first. Once we commit to doing His will, He grants us the knowledge, ability, and opportunity to create wealth.

Several years ago, the Holy Spirit spoke to me in the same manner that Jesus spoke to His followers. He revealed to me that I was failing to exercise faith. I was initially surprised by this disclosure because I was actively seeking God through His Word and felt that I was living all that I knew. I was a faithful member of the church and had accepted my personal call to ministry. I genuinely did my best to serve others, and I dedicated time to prayer and worship. However, an inner voice said to me, "Yes, you do all these things, and yet you still don't trust Me." I further examined God's Word and was convicted by the truth.

As I turned to God's Word, I realized that I was often consumed with anxiety. I worried about my mortgage. I worried about the business that my partner and I had founded and our financial woes. I worried about our church building project and the perceived lack of funding. I worried about material possessions and my family's long-term financial welfare. I essentially worried about all the things the Bible instructs us not to worry about. I worried to such a degree that I didn't really notice it. It was simply my way of life. I worried in the same fashion that I did when I didn't have a relationship with God. The revelation I received began a new season in my life—a season of introspection, growth, and testing. It also gave birth to this book project. I realized that the ultimate aim of faith is to enable trust in God. Mature faith should be synonymous with trust. In this section of the book, we will explore the less traveled road that leads to unfaltering trust in God.

Chapter 7

Taste and Seek

O taste and see that the Lord is good: blessed is the man that trusteth in Him. O fear the Lord, ye His saints: for there is no want to them that fear Him. The young lions do lack, and suffer hunger: but they that seek the Lord shall not want any good thing (Psalm 34:8-10 KJV).

The thirty-fourth Psalm is one of my favorite passages of Scripture where the psalmist begins by establishing the importance of praise, a subject we explore later in the text. The psalmist focuses on the benefits that we are afforded when we place our trust in God and rightly declares that those who trust God are blessed. In fact, God takes pride in rewarding those who demonstrate faithfulness to Him. God desires to use our lives as an example to attract others. While people readily associate God's blessing with material things, we should be wary of such limited thinking. The blessing of God results in things such as divine protection, spiritual vision, uncommon favor, supernatural timing, and yes, natural prosperity. God truly seeks to show His might through us and enable us to walk in Kingdom authority.

If God freely offers such benefits to those who seek His will, why do so few people enjoy an abundant life? As I pondered this question,

I considered my own life, and God revealed my tendency to become consumed with the cares of life. As I stated before, anxiety was my prior way of life. I realize now that this is the case for many believers. Most people, when confronted with the facts, readily admit that they have trouble exercising faith. I'm going to ask you to be brutally honest with yourself. How much time do you spend dreaming about the acquisition of material things? Do you worry about food, drink, shelter, or clothing? Are you tired of worrying about these things? Does the business of life crowd out your relationship with God, leaving little time for study, prayer, and meditation? Would you like to spend more time worshipping and less time worrying? If you're anything like me, I'm going to suggest that the solution to your worries begins with the question we asked in Chapter 4: In what or whom have you placed your hope?

Recall in Chapter 1 we established that hope is closely aligned with our desires. It's what we want God to bring to pass. In Chapter 4 we introduced the concept of *heavenly hope*, which aligns our desires with the will of God. Jesus' charge that we make God's will our first priority necessitates that our hope be placed in His eternal Kingdom. This is the essence of the Gospel message that is entrusted to all who believe in Christ. One of our greatest challenges as believers is keeping our focus squarely on the Kingdom of God. While ever so slight an infraction, it is easy to allow our focus to drift from the Kingdom, and by extension the King. We desire the things that the King provides but not necessarily His will.

When I really got honest with myself, I realized that my hope was not squarely focused on God's will. Unconsciously, I'd placed the things before the King. Maybe you've been in this position. Maybe you're in this position now. For most of us it is not a purposeful slight. It is just part of our maturation process as it relates to faith. The primary reason we find ourselves with false hope is because of our limited knowledge of God's Word and the principles that govern His Kingdom. The more we learn of God, the more we desire His will.

Truly Satisfying and Tastes Great

David invites us to taste or experience the goodness of God for ourselves. He states that those who fear God lack nothing. Fear in this context speaks to worship or reverence of God. Those who fear God respond to Him with obedience. This is the only acceptable response to God's Word. David contrasts those who fear God with those who lean to their own understanding by drawing an analogy with lions. Albeit swift by human standards, lions aren't very fast relative to their prey, yet they hunt some of the fastest animals in the wild. Lions compensate by utilizing cunning and teamwork. They see extremely well in the dark; they generally hunt at night; and they often hide near watering holes patiently waiting to surprise unsuspecting prey. Lions work as a team to stalk and surround their prey, which often includes stragglers or animals that are injured or sick. These methods allow lions to hunt large animals that ordinarily might overpower a single lion.

David observes that young lions are often hungry and suffer lack. This is a function of their immaturity. The young lions have little practical experience to draw on and thus are ruled by their appetites and instincts. Nevertheless, they quickly learn that they need more than good instincts and a healthy appetite to hunt successfully. Over time young lions gain valuable hunting experience, which in turn, produces patience and discretion. Young lions learn to appreciate the strength of the pride. Likewise, as we mature, we learn to trust in God, and it is through dependence on God that we overcome the cares of this world. It is also our dependence on God that assures our needs are met.

David learned from experience that the presence of God was both rewarding and addictive. Once you experience the presence of God, you naturally crave more. This is similarly true of God's Kingdom. Many people fail to seek God's Kingdom because they have never really tried it. What do I mean by that? It is common for people to spend much of their time consumed with worry and the cares of this world. We don't necessarily worry because we want to; we worry because of what we've been taught and what we've experienced. The world lives by principles such as "every man for himself" and "only the strong survive." We are taught independence from a very young age. We place our hope in things because that's what those before us did. However, we must learn to place our hope in the Kingdom of God, and we must learn to depend on God.

The Kingdom of God is an acquired taste. So while everyone is invited to try for themselves, many will forgo the offer. For many, the artificial confections of the world's system are more inviting than the sweet savor of God's Kingdom. Unfortunately, many miss out on the great supper promised in the Kingdom because they refuse to try it themselves. David invites us to taste and see for ourselves. We must apply the Word of God in our daily lives no matter how ridiculous it seems to others. It is then that we will experience the distinction between God's system and the system of the world. The Kingdom, like exquisite food, has exceptional quality. If you taste it, you will seek it. And when you seek it, what you need and more will be given to you. That's what happens when you're an heir of the King.

Two Pennies for Your Thoughts

He called His disciples to Him and said, "I assure you, this poor widow has given more than all the others have given. For they gave a tiny part of their surplus, but she, poor as she is, has given everything she has" (Mark 12:43-44 NLT).

Many of the recorded events of the final week of Jesus' earthly ministry took place in or around the temple at Jerusalem, where there were various receptacles placed for collections. There was also a treasury room near the women's court where worshippers could also contribute their offerings. During one of His visits to the temple, Jesus stood in this treasury room and observed those who came to present their offerings.

While He watched, a steady stream of individuals came and dropped their money into the receptacles, including several individuals who contributed large amounts of money to the temple treasury. Among this large crowd of people was a widow who dutifully came and dropped two mites or pennies into the receptacles. Although these two copper coins were the smallest denomination of currency available during that time, this offering represented the woman's entire livelihood. The woman is described as poor. The word "poor" used in this context meant impoverished or destitute. However, despite her low socioeconomic status, this woman did not pass up an opportunity to present her offering to the Lord.

Jesus then summoned His disciples in order to share His observations with them. He noted how during the time He'd observed the crowd, many individuals had contributed substantial amounts of money. Then pointing to the poor widow, He made a very interesting remark. He told His disciples that the poor widow had given more than all the other contributors He'd observed that day. I can imagine the perplexed look on the disciples' faces as they pondered Jesus' comment. After taking one look at the poor widow, they were likely eager to know how she could afford to make a significant contribution.

Jesus quickly shed light on His assessment. His valuation of the woman's generosity was not based on the absolute value of her contribution but rather the relative value. Presumably all the individuals who came before her had exceeded her donation in absolute terms. While others may have been impressed by sizable donations, Jesus took a different perspective. He noted that most of the people merely contributed a small portion of their abundance or wealth; He then contrasted this with the widow who gave everything she had. Her offering was distinguished because she had made a sacrifice. This type of giving—sacrificial giving—is the highest form of generosity.

This account further demonstrates that God's assessment of giving differs from ours. If we study Scripture closely, we find that God places greater value on our attitude in giving than He does on the amount of our gift. We noted in Chapter 6 that many people struggle in life because of their attitude in giving. While these individuals claim to trust God, they still give sparingly or not at all. Yet God requires those who serve Him to give liberally. This does not mean that we must give all that we have as the poor widow did; however, it does suggest we should be willing to make a sacrifice and not just give of our surplus. When we make a sacrifice in our giving, it shows that we place more trust in God than we do in ourselves or our possessions.

Jesus praised the woman because her sacrifice demonstrated a rare type of faithfulness. As we've noted before, Jesus regularly identified significant acts of faith. The widow's sacrifice may not be recognized as a great act of faith if viewed with an untrained eye. However, I challenge you to consider the context more thoroughly. This woman was impoverished and the extent of her livelihood was two mites. It's hard to translate that in today's terms, but it is believed that two mites may have been one sixteenth of a day's wage at that time. If you were down to your last bit of income, what would you do with it? While it's nice to believe that we all are as devoted as the poor widow, I'm reticent to believe that most people would go out and give it to the local church. Unless you understand principles that govern God's Kingdom, the widow's course of action simply seems ridiculous.

Recall that Jesus had chastised His followers on an earlier occasion because of their failure to trust God. This lack of faith was demonstrated by constant anxiety. Jesus characterized worry over things such as food, drink, clothing, or shelter as a failure to trust God's system. His implication was that the believer should trust God's system because God is aware of our daily needs. How pleased Jesus must have been to have actually found someone actively applying this type of faith. The poor widow must have hoped in something greater than herself when she so readily gave all that she had. The Bible records her unconventional act of faith as a testimony of what it means to place our hope in heavenly things.

TRY HIM FOR YOURSELF

The Bible provides no further record of the poor woman with the great faith. We are left to wonder what became of her. Because most of us are fond of storybook endings, we would like to believe that the woman's financial condition improved dramatically as a result of her generous gift. We have either been convinced or have convinced ourselves that God will afford us material things each time we give. However, that's simply not the way that God's system works. Remember faith involves acting without a guarantee. This is true with respect to giving as well as any other area of our life. We act on God's Word because we trust that He will do what's best for us. This is the type of faith the poor widow demonstrated. She made up her mind to taste and see for herself. I know that in the end her hope in God did not result in disappointment.

Now that we've examined this woman's account, you must ask yourself a question: How will your entry in the Book of Life be recorded? Will you look back over a life filled with worry and regret? Or will you have lived a life filled with the joy and peace that only God can offer? Will you live the abundant life that God has promised you? Or will you merely get by on whatever the system of the world affords you? Will you wander in a personal wilderness of hopelessness? Or will you trust God as He leads you into your promised land? The answer boils down to whether or not you are willing to accept David's invitation. You've got to taste and see for yourself. It doesn't matter that others have tried Him. As the apostle Paul suggests, we all have an individual race to complete (see Heb. 12:1). He understood that our motivation for the race we call life must be hope in God.

I must admit that I was quite apprehensive about placing my trust in God. I feel most comfortable with decisions that can be made by reasoning. Therefore, I consciously resist the inclination to lean to my own understanding. However, during my season of introspection, I began to prove God's Word. I applied those principles that in my mind seemed hard to believe, and I honestly and thoroughly examined my motives. For the first time in my life, I obeyed God simply because I wanted to please Him. I no longer conformed but was transformed in the area of faith. I was able to graduate from religion to a more personal relationship.

I discovered that there is a calming peace that comes from standing on God's Word regardless of the outcome. While there have been many times that I failed to acquire the outcome that I desired, I can honestly say that whenever I've placed my trust in God, I've consistently received the outcome I needed. I now have confidence that everything God allows, works for my benefit because I have surrendered my life to Him. I invite you to try Him for yourself—and I don't mean in a finicky sort of way. I invite you to take a seat at His table and try everything He has to offer. I will assure you that His offerings will keep you coming back for more. The more you taste of His goodness, the more you will seek His Kingdom.

Chapter 8

Hearing Is Believing

Verily, Verily, I say unto you, I am the door of the sheep. All that ever came before Me are thieves and robbers: but the sheep did not hear them. I am the door: by Me if any man enter in, he shall be saved, and shall go in and out, and find pasture (John 10:7b-9 KJV).

The events recorded in the seventh through the tenth chapters of John provide a detailed account of one of Jesus' more notable visits to Jerusalem. Jews from all over the region of Palestine had prepared to travel to Jerusalem to observe the Feast of Tabernacles (also known as the feast of booths or tents). The annual event was one of three prominent Jewish festivals and was highly anticipated. Virtually every Jewish family within 20 miles of the city would move out of their homes to live in tents that were constructed for the festival, which was done in remembrance of the nation of Israel's wilderness experience during which they lived in tents.

At this time, Jesus' reputation had spread rapidly throughout the region. However, not everyone was receptive to His ministry. In fact, many of the religious leaders in Jerusalem were threatened by His message and sudden rise to prominence. They feared that Jesus' influence would rival their own and unseat their authority over the people. Certain religious leaders even plotted against Jesus and challenged His authority. Although His family urged Him to make a public show of His ministry during the festival, Jesus initially went in secret, staying out of public view, thus allowing anticipation and debate about Him to build to a crescendo. The stage now set, He used the festival as an opportunity to declare the Gospel message and to distinguish Himself and His ministry.

When Jesus began to teach openly in the temple and around the city, predictably, He was challenged by members of the religious establishment who questioned whether He had been truly sent from God. Jesus then used a parable about a shepherd to distinguish Himself and His ministry from those who'd come before Him and those who would come after. In this illustration He alluded to Himself as the good shepherd and His followers as sheep. Jesus explained that when a shepherd merely calls his sheep by name, the sheep instinctively follow upon hearing their shepherd. The shepherd guides the sheep, leading them safely to pasture.

To appreciate the depth of Jesus' illustration, it is helpful to know a bit about Middle-Eastern sheep herding during that period. Sheep were usually kept in a fenced enclosure or even a cave. The enclosure was chosen because there was only one way in or out, and it was not uncommon for several shepherds to keep their sheep in the same enclosure. Sheep by their very nature are dependent animals. The shepherd would spend time with the sheep so that they would learn to recognize his voice and to trust only him. The sheep learned that the shepherd was the sustainer of life and thus followed the shepherd wherever he led.

The key point in this illustration is the link between the welfare of the sheep and their ability to recognize the voice of their shepherd. Interestingly enough, the sheep didn't actually need to physically see the shepherd. They simply would act based on what they heard. As it related to the flock, hearing and not seeing caused them to believe. Their intimate relationship with the shepherd resulted in a tremendous level of trust. The relationship between the sheep and their shepherd is an exclusive one. We learn that sheep will not follow the voice of a stranger. In fact, sheep instinctively retreat from a strange voice.

DOOR NUMBER ONE

In addition to the title of good shepherd, Jesus described Himself as the door of the sheepfold. Recall that the sheepfold was an enclosure with only one means of access. The enclosure, whether a fence or cave, did not generally have a physical door, so the shepherd many times would lay across the opening. The shepherd literally served as the doorway. In this way, the sheep could not wander astray, and predators were not allowed to enter and harm the sheep. This demonstrated the level of care that the shepherd provided the sheep. While others, such as an undershepherd, might have assisted with the caretaking of the flock, only the shepherd would go to the extreme of laying down his life for the sheep.

Jesus warned His followers that anyone who did not enter by the door was undoubtedly a thief and robber. Inasmuch as Jesus is the door, He is the only way to salvation. Any message contrary to this truth, regardless of how well-meaning, leads to danger and destruction. This is where belief comes into play. Recall that we said belief is exemplified by the confidence you have in the ability and word of another. In order to trust God, you must have knowledge of His Word. And in order to gain knowledge of His Word, you must learn to recognize His voice. The power of God is accessed through knowledge of His Word.

How then do we activate the power of God's Word? Paul ponders this very question in the tenth chapter of Romans. "How can we be saved except we believe?" he asks. "And how can we believe in the one who saves if we don't know His voice?" (Rom. 10:14, author's paraphrase). Paul clearly understands that our welfare is tied to our relationship with the Savior and Good Shepherd, Christ Jesus. However, he also understand that in order to enjoy the benefits of His care, we must both recognize and believe His Word. Paul concludes that faith is activated by adherence to the Word of God (see Rom. 10:17). If you are going to grow in faith, your knowledge must be translated into believing. The sheep in the illustration benefited because when the shepherd spoke, they didn't simply hear audibly; they responded! In fact, many times when we read the word hear in the Bible, it actually refers to our response. If you truly believe God, you will respond appropriately when you hear His Word.

STRANGE MEDICINE

Jesus heard that they had put him out, and finding him, He said, "Do you believe in the Son of Man?" He answered, "Who is He, Lord that I may believe in Him?" Jesus said to him, "You have both seen Him, and He is the one who is talking with you." And he said, "Lord, I believe." And he worshiped Him (John 9:35-38 NASB).

During His stay in Jerusalem for the Feast of Tabernacles, Jesus encountered a man who'd been blind from birth. His physical condition had relegated him to a life of begging, and he may well have been asking for alms when Jesus and the disciples came upon him. During their conversation, the disciples asked Jesus the reason for the man's physical infirmity, and they reasoned that either the man or his parents had sinned. In Jewish culture, sickness was generally associated with sin and was assumed divine punishment for disobedience of God's law.

Jesus explained that the man's condition was not a result of his sin or that of his parents. He said that the man had been born blind so that the power of God could be demonstrated through his life. This concept was surely difficult for the disciples to understand, for it hardly seems fair that this man had been blind from birth and relegated to the status of a beggar. These circumstances apply to many things we witness in our daily lives. It's certainly difficult to understand why people suffer with physical and mental handicaps, or why people suffer with terminal illness or disease. Like the disciples, we are at times unaware of God's ultimate plan.

The Bible does not suggest that there was much dialogue between Jesus and the blind beggar. In fact, we read of Jesus simply taking action. After speaking to His disciples, Jesus spat on the ground and made clay with His saliva. Next, He put the clay on the blind man's eyes and sent him to wash in a pool that was nearby. Jesus' actions seem unorthodox, to say the least; nonetheless, mixing clay with saliva was an actual practice used to treat eye infections. What was seemingly ridiculous was His application of the practice and not so much the practice itself. Jesus did not apply this rudimentary practice to treat an eye infection. Instead, He applied it to cure a man who had been blind from birth.

I wonder about the blind man's thoughts during this encounter. It is likely that the encounter may have begun with him asking for alms. If so, he certainly got more than he bargained for. Without the ability to see, the blind man was in many respects at the mercy of those around him. Sure, there were some things he may have learned to manage on his own, but his existence depended largely on the charity of others. This account suggests that the blind man knew little about Jesus and hadn't met Him prior to that occasion. I can hardly imagine his astonishment regarding what unfolded next.

Having assessed the man's condition, Jesus introduced him to His innovative brand of healthcare. Jesus instructed the blind man to do something that to most would seem laughable. Nevertheless, the blind man obeyed without question and immediately gained his sight. Belief is exemplified by the confidence we have in God's Word. We must comply regardless of how it compares with our experience or reasoning. The man acted on what he believed, and his small act of faith resulted in the miracle of gaining sight.

Believe It, or Not!

It is interesting to note the response of those who knew the blind beggar. Notice that hey did not witness the process he went through to receive his healing, only the final product. His neighbors and others began to ask was he indeed the same man. Even though they recognized his appearance, they could not believe the transformation that had taken place. The obvious transformation was the fact that the blind man could actually see; yet, just as important was the accompanying change in attitude. Having received his sight, he appeared outwardly and inwardly a new man.

This story is a metaphor of what happens when we place our confidence in God's Word. Miracles happen every day because lives are changed by the power of God's Word. When we believe God to the point that we obey His Word, we are transformed. Maybe you've had an experience similar to that of the blind man. The transformation effected by God's Word naturally causes a stir among those who are close to us. The miracle of change is just as influential as the miracle of sight. Our friends and family members ponder if we are the same person they used to know. But that's just it! We're not the same. If we believe God's Word, the truth not only sets us free from anything that has us bound; it also transforms us from the inside out. The blind man believed and received his sight. In what way do you desire to be made whole? Are you willing to believe God and obey His instructions? Recall from Chapter 2 that miraculous things are possible if you believe and obey God's Word.

In addition to his astonished family and friends, others had gotten wind of the blind man's miraculous healing. Similar to what they had heard about the crippled man near the Pool of Bethesda, the religious leaders began to also inquire about the man who had received his sight. They discovered that he too had been healed on the Sabbath. Again, we note a practical fact of life. Not everyone will be happy when change takes place in your life, because it often shines a light on their personal need for change. When the religious leaders questioned the man regarding his healing, they refused to accept his personal testimony as true and suggested the miraculous healing was a hoax. Their unrepentant attitude caused them to reject the truth that Jesus had indeed miraculously healed him. They even went as far as to summon his parents to ascertain if he had indeed been blind from birth.

With his parents and others attesting to the fact that the man had been born blind, the religious leaders summoned him a second time. At this point, they resorted to attempts to discredit Jesus as well as the blind man himself. However, the man grew increasingly confident in his testimony despite their persecution. The man told the religious leaders that whereas he was once hopelessly blind, he now had the ability to see. His personal transformation was his only testimony and his best defense against his detractors. As far as he was concerned, the man who'd healed him must have been sent from God.

The religious leaders were angered by the man's testimony and had him thrown out of the synagogue. Nonetheless, I believe that God was smiling at the conviction of the man who at that point had never seen Jesus. Hearing he'd been excommunicated from the synagogue, Jesus sought the man out. When He found him, He asked him a simple question: "Do you believe in the Son of God?" Jesus asked him that question because the man needed to know the object of his faith. Our faith must be founded in God's Word and the person of Jesus Christ. The man asked Jesus to point him to the Son of God so that he could believe in Him. Jesus then identified Himself, at which point the man fell down and worshipped Him. Although he'd been rejected by the establishment, he was graciously accepted into Christ's Kingdom. What a wonderful testimony of a man who could not see and yet believed.

A FAMILIAR VOICE

We began this chapter by establishing the link between belief and hearing the voice of God. However, just as the sheep in our example knew their shepherd's voice, you must also be able to distinguish the Good Shepherd's voice. There are a number of practical steps that we all can take to better familiarize ourselves with God's voice, but we must first understand the manner by which God communicates. I've learned over time that God communicates exclusively through His Word. It may come by different vehicles, but it all emanates from His Word. Whether it is through the Bible, His Spirit, or a human vessel, God simply reaffirms His Word.

The Bible is the perfect example of this principle. When you see the term "word" in the New Testament of the Bible, it is generally translated from two Greek words. *Logos* generally refers to a written expression or thought, and *rhema* generally refers to a thought that is verbally expressed. Much of the Bible is composed of logos or written Word. It is not written expressly to you or me; however, the principles of the Bible apply to everyone and everything under the authority of God. By contrast, promises apply to only believers.

God does not have to speak expressly to you as it involves a principle or promise because if you apply His written Word, the result comes automatically. God testifies of the surety of His own Word when He promises that it will not return to Him void but rather will accomplish what He intends (see Isa. 55:11). It is as if He speaks to you directly. Rhema, on the other hand, is generally associated with the Spirit of God or a vessel He uses to communicate directly. God may use a human vessel to speak expressly to you. Alternatively, He may communicate with you by His Spirit which speaks directly to a given situation in your life. Whatever the case, the message will always be consistent with His written Word.

If we understand the manner in which God communicates, we have valuable insight into distinguishing His voice. Although my list may not prove exhaustive, I have concluded that there are three practical things that we can do to better distinguish the voice of God. The first thing we must do is dedicate ourselves to studying the Word. What better way to familiarize yourself with God's voice than to immerse yourself in His written Word. God rarely communicates in an audible voice. As my pastor likes to say, He speaks in our thoughts. That dynamic brings with it an interesting challenge. You have to distinguish the voice or thoughts of God from your own. This is why the Bible attests that God's Word is sharper than a two-edged sword, dividing the soul from the spirit (see Heb. 4:12). By studying His written Word, we train ourselves to distinguish His voice when we hear it.

The second thing we must do is become an active part of the Church. Christ identifies Himself with the Church often referring to it as His Bride. The Church or assembly is the collection of believers chosen by Christ. Becoming a part of the Church is not as simple as adding your name to the rolls of a local congregation. If you are going to become part of the Church, you must become one with Christ. This means that you dedicate yourself to living according to His Word and you separate yourself for the work of Christ. When you make this commitment, you enjoy an intimate relationship with Christ and an intimate level of communication.

The third thing we must do is dedicate time to prayer. While this is a topic we will explore in much greater detail later in the text, I want to mention it in the context of recognizing the voice of God. Prayer is the time we set aside to communicate with God—*communicate* being the operative word. When most people think of prayer, they think of petitions. However, this is merely a small part of the equation. The most important part of prayer is the opportunity to receive instructions from God concerning our lives.

Once we become familiar with the voice of God, we have the confidence to act on His Word. Hearing does lead to believing. God speaks to us in order to teach us, encourage us, and guide us; however, we must believe what He says. This belief must be translated into action. The next time you hear the voice of God, be encouraged by the testimony of the blind beggar. Let your response be "Lord, I believe," and watch the miraculous change your belief produces.

CHAPTER 9

WIN, LOSE, OR DRAW

And He summoned the crowd with His disciples, and said to them,
"If anyone wishes to come after Me, he must deny himself, and take
up his cross and follow Me. For whoever wishes to save his life will
lose it, but whoever loses his life for My sake and the gospel's will save
it. For what does it profit a man to gain the whole world, and forfeit
his soul? For what will a man give in exchange for his soul?" (Mark
8:34-37 NASB).

During one of His ministry trips, Jesus summoned His disciples
and a crowd who had gathered, to teach them an important lesson on
faith, explaining the level of commitment required of His followers.
It's important to note that the offer to follow Christ is an open invitation. Nevertheless, there is a duty imposed if you choose this lifestyle.
The cost of discipleship is obedience. Jesus further explained that in
order to follow Him, you must deny yourself. Christ must be in control, and your will must take a back seat. There is no place in your
heart for selfishness because your chief responsibility is serving others.
Service is often synonymous with sacrifice. It is also the key to greatness in Christ's Kingdom.

Jesus presented an interesting paradox in the human life. He said those who wish to preserve their lives must lose them for His sake. As believers, we must dedicate our lives to serving Christ and spreading the Gospel of His Kingdom. We cannot simply live as we choose. Instead, we must give ourselves to Christ in the same manner that He gave Himself for us. Practically speaking, we must obey God's Word to the point that His character is produced in us. Following his conversion, the apostle Paul stated that he no longer lived for himself; Christ, in effect, lived through him (see Gal. 2:20). People around us come to know Christ and His great love because we demonstrate it in our daily lives, which requires a significant sacrifice on our part. And in order to accomplish this, we must place the welfare of others ahead of our own. We must also discipline ourselves to respond to people and circumstances based on God's Word and not how we feel. This type of attitude is achieved only when we adopt an eternal focus.

Jesus also explained the consequences of declining His invitation. Anyone who chooses not to obey God in this present life loses the gift of eternal life. While this gift of eternal life is free to all who accept Christ as Lord, it does cost us to preserve our eternal life. The cost, as Jesus explained, is your present life. This is why Jesus asked how one can benefit if he gains an abundance of the material things this world offers, yet forfeits his own soul (see Mark 8:36). The soul is the immortal part of our being. In essence, we each are extended an invitation to spend eternity with God. Whether or not you truly accept His invitation boils down to what or in whom you place your trust.

We began this section of the book by talking about the necessity of making God's will our priority. In order to retain eternal life, we must be willing to abandon temporal possessions, ungodly relationships, and carnal thinking. When we learn of God's Kingdom, we come to understand that earthly sacrifice results in eternal gain. Conversely, misplaced trust in worldly possessions, relationships, or thinking may result in eternal loss. The apostle Paul understood this paradox. In reflecting on his stature, possessions, and accomplishments, he considered them worthless when compared to the privilege of a personal relationship with Christ Jesus (see Phil 3:8). There is nothing that compares to the value of one's life. That is why Jesus was willing to sacrifice His earthly life in exchange for our eternal lives. Now the question is posed to each one of us. What will we give in exchange for eternal life? If Christ is our example, the choice is clear.

READY TO DIE

Father, if You are willing, take this cup from Me; yet not My will, but Yours be done. An angel from heaven appeared to Him and strengthened Him (Luke 22:42-43 NIV).

In the days leading up to His crucifixion, Jesus traveled with His disciples to Jerusalem. The wonderful reception He received on what is commemorated as Palm Sunday was hardly a predictor of events that would transpire. However, Jesus was well aware of why He'd come to Jerusalem. Moreover, He was painfully aware of the fate that He was about to suffer. He had already told His disciples of the things that He would have to endure on several occasions; nevertheless, the impending event was far from their minds. Jesus, sensing the time of His betrayal was at hand, arranged to eat the Passover meal with His disciples two days prior to the official observance.

A somber mood was undoubtedly pervasive during the meal that Jesus shared with His disciples, and when He explained to them that the hour of His suffering had arrived, He also revealed that someone from among this chosen group would betray Him. The level of faith that Jesus displayed in this respect is beyond comprehension. He was aware that Judas would betray Him, yet He accepted this betrayal because of His trust in the sovereign plan of God. It must have pained Him to know that someone He deeply loved would betray Him. It likely pained Him even more knowing the unbearable suffering that Judas would inflict on himself. In any case, Jesus never deviated from God's plan, regardless of the personal cost.

Upon hearing this news, the disciples were distressed and troubled at Jesus' revelation. Although He'd predicted His death previously, the imminent nature of His revelation began to settle in. Consequently, Jesus began to comfort them, telling them that He was going to prepare a place for them. Although His present ministry was drawing to a close, He was returning to Heaven to intercede for them with the Father. He also reminded them of the promise of the Holy Spirit, which He referred to as a comforter. The Holy Spirit would go alongside them as they perpetuated His ministry and spread the Gospel of the Kingdom. After encouraging them for some length, Jesus prayed for His disciples and the countless generations of believers who would believe through their testimony.

NOT MY WILL

Following supper, Jesus and His disciples left the upper room and went to a garden called Gethsemane, located east of Jerusalem on the Mount of Olives. This Garden was a place where Jesus and His disciples had often met, and it appears that Jesus wanted those closest to Him to support Him there in this time of great sorrow. Judas had previously departed, and Jesus had decided to take Peter, John, and James along with Him to pray. Although He separated Himself a short distance, He admonished these three disciples to pray as well. We should take note of Jesus' actions during this extremely challenging situation. One of the first things we observe is that He engaged other believers for support. Even among the disciples there was an inner circle, and during this pivotal time, He selected the members of His inner circle to support Him. More importantly, Jesus separated Himself and prayed. Jesus did not seek counsel from others concerning His decision, nor did He lean to His own understanding. He sought God for His will concerning the situation.

Jesus knew that His accusers would soon arrive. He also knew that the only way they could take Him is if He went willingly. In essence, the decision was up to Him. He knew that He would have to endure a most heinous manner of suffering and degradation, and the Bible tells us that the anticipation of His plight made Him sorrowful even to the point of death. Jesus then prayed to the Father concerning His plight. His petition may seem surprising when we consider that He asked the Father to deliver Him from His plight of suffering. However, we must understand that Jesus was uniquely both God and man. He had to endure the same emotions and mental anguish that we endure at trying times. We observe His human nature inasmuch as He wished to avoid the suffering that was ahead of Him. Who among us wouldn't have asked the same thing? The strength of His faith was not demonstrated by what He requested, but rather by His resolve in the face of such dire circumstances.

This example is critically important to our understanding of faith. Jesus was well aware of His fate yet asked to change it. While it seems evident that His course would not be altered, Jesus was persistent in His plea. The Bible tells us that He sought God three times, praying more fervently each occasion. While it is not explicitly stated, it is apparent that Jesus received an answer to His petition. However, it was not the response He desired. Even so, Jesus accepted the will of God, despite His personal desire to forgo the plight laid before Him. He demonstrated that prayer is coming into agreement with God. (We will examine prayer more thoroughly in Chapter 14.) More importantly, He demonstrated the level of trust that we must place in God inasmuch as He was willing to entrust God with His life.

There is another subtle but important nuance to consider. The moment Jesus affirmed His choice to accept God's will, something incredible happened. An angel from Heaven appeared and strengthened Him—after one of His disciples had betrayed Him, many of the others had not been mature enough to come along, and His inner circle had literally fallen asleep on the job. There will be times when your closest confidants aren't able to support you. At these times, it's reassuring to know that God is always there. The second Jesus resolved to do God's will, He no longer had to rest in His own strength. God sent an angel to strengthen Him. God does the same thing in our lives. When we accept God's will in spite of our circumstances, He gives us the strength to carry it through.

"Not My will, but Yours be done" is the greatest declaration of faith in the history of mankind. It gives us a clear understanding of what it means to trust God. Our relationship with God does not guarantee that He will grant all our petitions. What parent gives their child whatever he or she desires? If we obey God, we have confidence that God not only hears us when we call, but that He will do what's best for us. Jesus was willing to subjugate His personal desire to accomplish God's will. His faith and ultimate sacrifice changed the world forever. Jesus could have chosen a lesser course of action, but He trusted God instead. His faith in God changed the world as we know it. What indelible mark does God plan for you to leave on the world through the exercise of faith?

THE LIFE YOU SAVE

The exercise of faith is far more than a mental exercise. God's way of thinking is not comparable to the way we think. It often requires faith for us to accept God's way of thinking. True faith rejects the notion that life will go according to the plan that we devise. True faith is also not based on our personal assessment of an outcome. Faith is a resolve that win, lose, or draw, we are committed to doing God's will. No matter the cost or the outcome, we will obey God's Word. That type of resolve comes only through the power of the Holy Spirit. Jesus' example demonstrates that God can and will give us the strength we need to carry us through whatever circumstances we encounter.

We began this chapter by discussing Jesus' call to discipleship, and we learned that discipleship is costly. The Word of God says that we should make our bodies a living sacrifice (see Rom. 12:1). It further states that a holy or set-apart life is the only sacrifice that is truly acceptable to God. God loved you and me so much that He gave His life in exchange for ours. Therefore, the only acceptable exchange is a gift in kind. What else can we offer the God of the universe who owns everything? You are God's greatest creation, and He gave you the greatest gift of all—a free will. Your will is the only thing you have that is exclusively yours. Everything else belongs to God. If you truly trust God, you will give your life to Him by subjecting your will to His. It is the greatest thing you have to give.

While Jesus explained that discipleship is costly, He also spoke of the great benefits that accrue to those who put their trust in Him.

Jesus said that God will reward those who faithfully follow Him. I encourage you to place your complete trust in Him and see if He won't exceed your greatest expectations. Although we have only one life to give, God owns everything this world has to offer. If you are willing to lose your life for Christ's sake, the eternal life that you save will be your own. I pray you gain strength in the Lord as you submit to His will.

PART IV
LEARNING TO STAND

LEARNING TO STAND

Why art thou cast down, O my soul? and why art thou disquieted
within me? hope in God: for I shall yet praise Him, who is the health
of my countenance, and my God (Psalm 43:5 KJV).

King David is easily one of the most recognizable characters in the
Bible. The account of his valiant defeat of Goliath, as we discussed in
the Introduction of this book, has inspired individuals of all walks of
life for centuries. But while David is inextricably linked to his triumph
over the menacing giant, his contribution to the tapestry of faith can
hardly be eclipsed with this single episode. In fact, David's life plays
out as one of the most sensational dramas of biblical record. David's
odyssey spans the spectrum of the human experience ranging from
great triumph to stark tragedy. And through these various peaks and
valleys of his life, David was a man who remained faithful to God.
This characteristic, more than any other, distinguished him in the eyesight of God.

David is affectionately referred to as a man after the heart of God. He was by no means perfect; however, no one who has studied his life can question his unfeigned love for God. In fact, David's love for God resulted in an almost reckless brand of faith. His faith was epitomized not so much by his military conquests or his ascension to the throne; instead, it was exemplified by his intimate relationship with God which resulted in an uncompromised level of trust. David's faith not only resulted in courageous exploits, but it enabled him to stand firm in areas where most others fail. David learned to trust God during the most trying times of his life. He learned to love God's judgment, accept His chastisement, and submit to His will. It seems that when David's circumstances turned for the worse, he instinctively turned to God.

A great majority of the Book of Psalms is ascribed to David. Through his songs we peer into the heart of a man who was deeply devoted to God, and we find that many of these songs were composed during trying times. The forty-third Psalm is a glaring example. In this short stanza, David entreats God to deliver him from the devices of evil people. He speaks of suffering unjustly, and there is a sense of anguish regarding his situation. David admits that he is struggling with inner turmoil and is deeply saddened; yet in the midst of it all, David encourages himself through the affirmation of his hope in God. David knows that despite his situation, God is able to deliver him. David's resolve mirrors one of our key conclusions from Chapter 1— hope in God does not fail!

There is a subtle yet vital point that must not be overlooked here. David's statement in verse 5 holds the key to overcoming the mentally and emotionally unsettling times of life. He decides that in spite of his mental and emotional state, he will offer praise to God. To the human mind, this conclusion does not make sense. In fact, it seems flat-out ridiculous. Why should you praise God when you encounter tough times? The Latin root for the word *praise* expresses value. Therefore, praise, an act of your free will, demonstrates to God the value you place on your relationship with Him. It is an open invitation for God to commune with you.

Nothing pleases God more than genuine praise. It makes God feel like making His presence known. And when you and I are going through dire times, there is nothing we need more than the presence of God. When we truly appreciate David's example and respect God's point of view, we don't mind offering God ridiculous praise—the kind of praise that sets our souls at liberty because we have given up and given in to God! If we offer that kind of praise, there is little doubt that we will stand during the tough times, for we are no longer trusting in our own strength. Instead, we stand through the strength of God who lives inside us. I pray that this section of the book enlightens and encourages you as you learn to persevere through the trying times of life.

CHAPTER 10

WHEN YOU'RE LOSING HOPE

For we are saved by hope: but hope that is seen is not hope: for what a man seeth, why doth he yet hope for? But if we hope for that we see not, then do we with patience wait for it (Romans 8:24-25 KJV).

In Chapter 4, we introduced the concept of *heavenly hope*, a hope in God and His Kingdom that distinguishes followers of Christ. We further noted that the apostle Paul dealt extensively with this subject in his letter to the Romans. Paul assures believers that if we endure persecution for Christ's sake in this present life, we will reign with Him in His eternal Kingdom (see Rom. 8:17). Although we have the Holy Spirit as a foretaste of our future glory, we naturally desire to be relieved of the pain and suffering we encounter in this life. After all, hope is an expectation of a better future reality.

Paul gives us valuable advice for coping with the times when hope seems altogether lost. He says that our hope in God has the power to save us from drowning in a sea of hopelessness. Hope by definition looks beyond temporal circumstances; nevertheless, we must accept that it is not always easy to be hopeful, because the answers to problems are not always apparent and the end to suffering is not always in clear view. Paul says that at those times we must hope for what we cannot see. In other words, we must accept that God has promised us a wonderful future reality that greatly overshadows any present suffering. Paul identifies patience as a key requirement for exercising hope and faith. Patience is essential to persevering through tough times. If our hope is truly eternal, it is demonstrated by our patience.

NOT NOW, SON!

As I've matured in the area of faith, I've learned to appreciate the necessity of patience, for it is easy to get ahead of God when we let our emotions get the best of us. I can recall many occasions when I felt that God did not act in a timely fashion only to later discover that He acted just at the appropriate time. I've learned that faith means trusting God for both the how and the when. In addition, there have been numerous occasions when my lack of maturity prevented God from acting. Patience is essential because it develops character and causes us to mature. This is why I define patience as the proper investment of time. God ensures that we are mature enough to proceed to our next promotion. He also ensures that we are able to manage the things that He places in our care. When things feel bad on the outside, it is often evidence that God is working on the inside.

God deals with us in much the same way that any parent deals with a child. One of the toughest things for a small child to accept is waiting. Children live in the moment. They want, and often expect, immediate gratification. As such, they don't always respond well when they are required to wait. I have two young sons that provide me with plenty of firsthand experience in this area. By their way of thinking, "not now" might as well mean never. Sometimes they wait, albeit impatiently. Occasionally, their emotions get the best of them and they throw tantrums. They behave in this manner because of their immaturity. At their tender ages, they don't always understand that I am acting in their best interest. However, the more experience we have with one another, the better they understand my motives. My preschooler understands better than my toddler. He has a better grasp on the fact that in most instances I haven't denied his reward; I'm simply reserving it for the appropriate time. I teach him to wait with patience, and ultimately he receives everything that I've promised him. Does this type of relationship sound familiar?

God showed me how my dynamic with Him is similar to the one I have with my children. As Father, He knows what's best for me. Although there are many instances when I want Him to act immediately, He often impresses upon me the need to exercise patience. Like children we may have expectations that are ill-timed or ill-advised. The key is maturing to the point that we refrain from acting outside of God's will. Disobedience brought about by impatience annuls the promises of God; hence, the Bible encourages us to develop certain character traits to work alongside our faith. One of the chief among these traits is patience (see 2 Pet. 1:6). Patience allows the love and character of Christ to be perfected in us, and it is this perfecting or maturing process that prepares us for the things that God has in store for us through faith.

It is difficult to keep our focus on God during trying times and all the more challenging to wait with patience. Yet the Bible promises us that those who wait upon the Lord will be strengthened (see Isa. 40:31). As we noted before, hope in God does not disappoint, for God knows exactly what we need and knows when we need it. If we entrust our lives to Him, He never requires us to carry any load that we cannot bear. Nevertheless, we are required to place our hope in His eternal Kingdom. When the circumstances of life cause you to feel as though you are losing hope, remember this one thing: Your present suffering cannot compare to the glory in store for you when you reign with Christ in His manifested Kingdom. Hope in God gives you access to His Kingdom in this life and the one to come.

WHOM THE SON MAKES FREE

When Jesus saw her, He called her forward and said to her, "Woman, you are set free from your infirmity." Then He put His hands on her, and immediately she straightened up and praised God (Luke 13:12-13 NIV).

Jesus had been teaching in a synagogue on a Sabbath day when He noticed a woman who was bent double and unable to stand up straight. Her physical infirmity had been caused by an evil spirit, and as such, there was no medical remedy for her condition. We learn that the woman had suffered with this infirmity for 18 years. This woman in all likelihood was a faithful member of the synagogue, and those present had undoubtedly seen her on numerous occasions. Yet, people will often overlook those who suffer from physical or spiritual infirmities. If you suffer from an infirmity long enough, it simply becomes commonplace to you and to those around you. However, Jesus had compassion when He saw the woman, and it wouldn't be long until He was moved to action.

The Bible gives few details about the woman save her debilitating condition. Her participation in the synagogue service suggests she was a devout Jew, whereas many individuals in her position might have given up on worship altogether. Nonetheless, it appears that she was faithful in seeking God. Maybe it was her lot in life to bear such a difficult burden, or maybe she had an inner strength that sustained her until the time that her Savior arrived.

In any case, it is important to note that the woman was not born with her infirmity; she knew what it was like to move about uninhibited, which likely made her condition even more untenable. How would you handle a similar situation? Maybe you're going through a comparable situation right now. This type of condition might easily cause an individual to lose hope, become angry, bitter, or depressed. However, we can learn a great lesson from the woman with the crooked back. Despite her seemingly hopeless condition, she remained faithful. There was something inside her that was greater than her present circumstances. I believe that something was her hope in God.

We noted earlier that Jesus took notice of the woman. While we can be certain that He observed the woman's physical condition (the Bible tells us that Jesus is touched by our infirmities—see Heb. 4:15), He also perceived much more. If you look closely at people, their faces often tell a story. Sometimes you can literally see the emotional scars of life that have

prescription we need for any circumstance we encounter in life. His Spirit provides the gentle reminder we need to keep us from going astray. The Word is meant to be our guide and the Holy Spirit is meant to be our tutor (see John 14:26).

The Holy Spirit also intercedes for us in prayer. In Chapter 9, we noted that prayer is the time to seek God's will or receive instructions. Paul notes that in trying times we may not know what we should pray or feel incapable of praying altogether. However, if we yield ourselves to God, His indwelling Spirit actually prays on our behalf (see Rom. 8:27). This underscores the vital importance of prayer. God does not simply leave it to our human intellect; He is able to work through us to interject His will in the earth through the ministry of the Holy Spirit. We need only submit our will to Him. Prayer does wonders for the soul. There have been many occasions when I have felt down only to have my soul encouraged through communion with God. It is so good to know that God cares about me so much that He put in a safeguard to keep the lines of communication open. The Holy Spirit further sustains my hope in God through the awesome power of prayer.

Contrary to popular belief, strong men don't always prevail, and intelligent men don't always get rich. After going through a very difficult time in his life, Job described life as short and full of trouble (see Job 14:1). Likewise, King Solomon mused over the unpredictability of life. Unexpected circumstances befall all men (see Eccl. 9:11). In these two cases, it is important to note that both these men enjoyed a relationship with God. Their observations give credence to the assertion of placing our hope in God. We must never allow hard times or unexpected events to diminish our hope in God. While this life is both challenging and short, God offers us eternal life with Him. And while life is indeed unpredictable, God never changes and His Word is sure. Our faith in God does not lead to a detour around the rough terrain of life. His Spirit gives us the endurance to pass over those roads instead. The question is not if, but when will difficult times arise. The key to success in life is placing our trust in God and allowing Him to prepare us for whatever roads may lie ahead.

Paul came to an important conclusion that aided him greatly in completing the course that God had set before him. He realized that God ultimately causes the circumstances of life to benefit those who hope in Him (see Rom. 8:28). Though we encounter trouble, persecution, and even calamity, God's love is ever present. Paul reassures us that nothing that occurs in this life can separate us from God's love. His love, manifested through His Spirit, enables us to overcome any obstacle that we face. When you feel as though you are losing hope, consider how much God loves you. He loves you so much that He created an entire world just for you and entrusted it to your care. He loves you so much that when you lost your life, He paid an unimaginable price to restore you. He loves you so much that even though He makes His home in Heaven, He sent a part of Himself to live inside of you. His love is never far from you, because His Spirit and His Kingdom are close to your heart. Those who love God are distinguished by the fact that they never lose hope (see 1 Cor. 13:7). Through patience we express our love for God, and dutifully place our trust in Him.

CHAPTER 11

WHEN YOU FIND IT HARD TO BELIEVE

Jesus said to him, "Because you have seen Me, have you believed? Blessed are they who did not see, and yet believed." Therefore many other signs Jesus also performed in the presence of the disciples, which are not written in this book; but these have been written so that you may believe that Jesus is the Christ, the Son of God; and that believing you may have life in His name (John 20:29-31 NASB).

In Chapter 9, we discussed the events leading up to Jesus' crucifixion and recalled that Jesus took great care to prepare His disciples for what was about to take place. He focused their attention on the work that lay ahead, making plans to meet His close companions following His resurrection. Though Jesus promised He would rise again on the third day, His disciples did not believe Him. Thus, His crucifixion overwhelmed them with fear and shattered their faith. Even the loyal women who went to His grave to anoint His body did not expect to see Him alive. Yet that is exactly what happened. He rose on the third day just as He had promised.

Afterwards, Jesus sent word for His apostles to meet Him as previously instructed. However, if the loyal women had not brought them a firsthand account, their unbelief might have prevented them from being reunited with their Lord. The disciples had been fearing for their lives and were uncertain about their future, yet if they were ever to boldly preach the gospel of His Kingdom, the truth of the resurrection had to be settled in their mind.

When Jesus first appeared to His apostles shortly after His resurrection, Thomas was inexplicably absent from the group. He did return, but not until Jesus had already departed. Despite the eyewitness account shared by His close companions, Thomas still refused to believe that Jesus had indeed risen from the dead, and he vowed that unless he had physical evidence he would never believe.

Despite a close personal relationship that had evolved over three years, Thomas did not believe the promise he'd personally received from Christ. And his position did not change even after hearing the firsthand account of his fellow companions. Thomas demanded evidence, and he would not be satisfied until he could see with his own eyes and feel with his own hands. Thomas' attitude is characteristic of so many believers today. When God's Word doesn't line up with our limited knowledge or personal experience, we refuse to believe. This is not to imply that Thomas was a bad person; he simply needed to be strengthened in the area of faith.

It is not always easy to believe God's Word. Just examine the numerous examples provided in the Bible. Nonetheless, it is imperative that we discipline ourselves to abide by God's Word. This is especially true when it challenges our way of thinking. We must understand that God's Word defies conventional wisdom and human experience. However, belief in God's Word actually transforms our lives. It breaks down the artificial constraints we have placed on our mind, the very hindrances that prevent us from thinking and acting like God.

I've come to realize that unbelief reveals the weak areas in my relationship with God. Whereas, our relationship with God is strengthened through praise, worship, and prayer. If we are lax in these areas, we naturally struggle to accept God's Word, and the struggle that takes place in our minds is evidence that our faith is being tested. Acceptance of God's Word, on the other hand, is the product of spiritual maturity and is achieved through personal experience with God. Notice that I said experience with God, and not simply life experience. You can live an entire life and not truly know God. Yet, each time we accept God's Word in an unfamiliar or uncomfortable circumstance, it gives us the confidence we need to tackle our next test in life. The times when we find it hard to believe are the times that our faith is being perfected.

BELIEVE IT OR NOT

Jesus said unto her, I am the resurrection, and the life: he that believeth in Me, though he were dead, yet shall he live: and whosoever liveth and believeth in Me shall never die. Believest thou this? (John 11:25-26 KJV).

Jesus had many loyal followers aside from the twelve disciples whom He had selected to be special messengers. Among these followers were two faithful sisters, Mary and Martha, who lived in Bethany, a small village about two miles outside of Jerusalem. The sisters supported Jesus' ministry; and as a guest at their home on several occasions, Jesus developed a close relationship with them as well as with their brother, Lazarus, who Scripture describes as someone who Jesus cared for dearly.

On one occasion while traveling with His disciples, Jesus received word from the two sisters that Lazarus was very ill. Although there are limited details regarding his illness, we understand that his condition was grave. The sisters were very concerned about their brother and hopeful that Jesus would quickly come to see about His dear friend. However, when Jesus received word of Lazarus' condition, His response likely surprised those around Him. Jesus remarked that Lazarus' sickness would not end in death, despite reports that he was terminally ill. Jesus explained that God would be glorified through his sickness, and He continued with the business at hand.

Those acquainted with the situation were undoubtedly aware of the personal relationship Jesus shared with the family, and they likely expected an immediate response from Jesus. Even Jesus may have personally felt compelled to see about His friend; however, He always deferred to the plan of God. And Jesus knew that God's hand was working behind the scenes. God planned to use the situation as an opportunity to glorify His Son. Although the situation looked bleak, Jesus trusted God's will concerning His dear friend Lazarus.

Two days after receiving the message about Lazarus, Jesus informed the disciples that they were going to Bethany to wake Lazarus from his slumber. The disciples, being unaware that Lazarus had died, began to question His instructions, and so Jesus told them plainly that Lazarus was dead. Jesus further explained that Lazarus' death would provide an opportunity for their faith to be strengthened. Although the disciples had witnessed Jesus perform many miracles, His plan concerning Lazarus was very hard for them to believe.

Lazarus was no longer terminally ill but had died, and Jesus was a few days' journey from Bethany. Further complicating the situation was the fact that the Jewish leaders had tried to kill Jesus the last time He was in the region. By the disciples' reasoning, Jesus was putting His life as well as their lives in mortal danger to tend to a man who was beyond saving. The thought of waking a dead man from slumber was a difficult one to comprehend.

We must understand that God often works this way in our lives. While it is natural to have certain expectations of God, faith demands that we defer to His will. While others were distressed, Jesus rested on the fact that Lazarus' ultimate end was in God's hands. We must likewise believe that God is in control of everything that affects our lives. While it may be difficult to grasp everything that occurs in our lives, God's unconditional love for us should compel us to believe. As we noted before, belief is more about acceptance than comprehension. My childhood pastor use to say, "Faith doesn't make sense...and sense doesn't make faith." It was his way of telling us that we would not always comprehend the plan of God. Belief is not about figuring God out; belief is about accepting God's Word, because His Word never fails.

WAKING THE DEAD

When Jesus arrived in Judea, Lazarus had already been in the grave four days, and when Martha heard that Jesus was near, she immediately went to meet Him. Mary, however, remained in the house and mourned. Martha was naturally despondent over the death of her brother, and she told Jesus that if He had arrived sooner, her brother would not have died. Yet Martha still expressed a glimmer of hope. She knew that God would honor Jesus' word regardless of how the situation appeared. When Jesus comforted Martha and assured her that her brother would rise again, she readily assumed that Jesus was referring to the day of resurrection or eternal life. She never considered that her brother might live again in this present world. Jesus then confirmed her belief in the day of resurrection stating that He was the way to eternal life. However, Jesus had an immediate plan that Martha had yet to comprehend.

Jesus instructed Martha to summon her sister, Mary, for He desired to encourage her just as He had Martha. Meanwhile, Mary's actions indicated that she had given up on the situation. While there is no shame in mourning the death of a loved one, we must remember that in these times we must follow Martha's example and run to God. There are times in life when only God can provide the comfort we need. We must believe that He knows our troubles and more importantly, He can see us through them. As we stated earlier, amazing things happen when we believe; nevertheless, we will encounter times when it is hard to believe.

When Mary saw Jesus, she fell to His feet and began to weep. Those who accompanied her also began to weep. She then expressed the same concern as her sister, suggesting that her brother would have lived had Jesus arrived earlier. At this point, Jesus was moved to tears by the outpouring of grief over His dear friend Lazarus. He wasn't crying because Lazarus was dead, for He knew what He would do concerning Lazarus. Instead, Jesus felt empathy for the sisters because of their grieving. And as Jesus wept with the sisters, others who were gathered began to question His actions and accused Him of forsaking a man whom He loved. Consequently, Jesus was troubled not by their criticism, but their lack of faith in God.

Jesus then accompanied Mary and Martha to the tomb of Lazarus, and when He arrived, He instructed that the stone be rolled away from the tomb. When Martha heard His instructions, she questioned Jesus, expecting the corpse to have begun to decay by that time and warned that the smell would likely be terrible because he'd been dead four days. Jesus reminded Martha of His promise to raise Lazarus from the dead if she would believe. Recall it was Martha who declared that God would give Jesus whatever He asked. Jesus was prepared to ask God for what Martha might have considered unthinkable. Was Martha ready for a miracle?

Jesus began to pray aloud for the benefit of those present, because He wanted them to recognize the great miracle that was about to take place so that they would know that He had been sent by the Father. After praying to the Father, Jesus called Lazarus from the grave. Immediately Lazarus' spirit came back to his body, and he emerged from the tomb wearing grave clothes. Jesus instructed those present to remove those clothes and let him go. Imagine the amazement of those who were present. A man who had been in the grave four days was brought back to life. Truly God was glorified and the faith of Jesus' followers was greatly strengthened.

Life After Death

Raising Lazarus from the dead is regarded as the greatest miracle Jesus performed during His earthly ministry. The prospect of resuscitating a man who had been dead four days simply boggles the mind. I'm convinced that was the point. Jesus certainly could have laid hands on Lazarus and healed him from whatever ailed him. His followers had witnessed Him perform this task countless times. We noted in Chapter 3 that Jesus had revived another person who had died—a young girl; however, she had only recently died and was still lying in her bedroom when He arrived. But Lazarus was a different story altogether. Lazarus wasn't simply given up for dead; He'd been buried. There was no hope or expectation that Lazarus would live again. Even when Jesus Himself suggested it, His closest followers found it too hard to believe. Yet the power of God transcends all things, even death.

Through Lazarus, Jesus demonstrated that there is life after death. He showed the entire world that when everyone has given up on you, God can still resurrect you from a physical or spiritual grave. Death in a spiritual sense is separation from God who is our source. If we understand this, we recognize that the miracle referred to above happens every day. The Bible tells us that if we simply believe the testimony that Jesus was resurrected from the dead and accept Him as Lord, we are delivered from death and have a right to eternal life (see Rom. 10:9). That is what it means to be saved or delivered—to be set free from sin and given the right to eternal life. However, it happens only if we believe.

Belief encompasses more than just verbal acknowledgement. In fact, the term "confession" that is often used in the Bible means to acknowledge God's Word as true and agree to abide by it. Belief is not limited to a mental exercise. It influences who you are and what you stand for. When you realize this, you understand that it is not always easy to believe because your belief will be challenged. God desires that our confidence in Him exceed that which we place in anything else. That is why the Bible gives us testimonies of people who believed in seemingly impossible circumstances. Jesus believed in God where others failed, and as a result, Lazarus got a second lease on life.

Jesus commanded Lazarus to come forth from the grave, and his spirit returned to his body. While it is true that Jesus had unmatched authority in the earth, He always exercised that authority in concert with God's will. God desired that Lazarus be brought back to life so that men would glorify Him, and Jesus expressed complete confidence in His plan resulting in the miracle recorded in Scripture. We should likewise aspire to know the heart of God so that we can boldly declare His will. It is then that we can truly speak His Word with authority and know that the word we speak will come to pass. The account of Lazarus demonstrates the power of our words when aligned with God's will. We will discuss this principle in greater detail in Chapter 15.

Maybe you are finding it difficult to accept God's Word concerning the situation you're presently in. Maybe you feel as though your career, business, marriage, or ministry has been damaged beyond repair. Remember, the Word of God is a spring of life that can resurrect the gravest situations. The distinguishing aspect of the Gospel message is that it promises life after death. This is true with respect to the resurrection and eternal life. However, it is similarly true with respect to the situations we face in our daily lives. God calls upon us to believe the truths that are found in His Word. He is fully aware that the circumstances of life often make it challenging for us to accept these truths because it does not appear that they will come to pass. But keep in mind the words that He told Thomas—blessed are those who believe His Word in spite of how things seem.

The eyes of the Lord do search the earth looking for someone who He can use mightily. God would love nothing more than that someone to be you. However, you must believe God when others refuse to. You must believe God when circumstances make it difficult to do so. You must believe God when your emotions are fighting against you. You must believe God even when it doesn't seem to make sense. That type of belief causes you to act in faith, and genuine acts of faith call for a response from God. God truly blesses those who act on what they believe.

CHAPTER 12

WHEN YOU FEEL LIKE GIVING UP

A final word: Be strong with the Lord's mighty power. Put on all of God's armor so that you will be able to stand firm against all strategies and tricks of the devil (Ephesians 6:10-11 NLT).

Along the routes of his three missionary journeys, Paul had established many local assemblies. Prominent among these was the church at Ephesus, which Paul had established at the conclusion of his second missionary journey. Paul later sojourned at Ephesus for nearly three years during his third and final missionary journey.

Ephesus was the capital of the Roman province of Asia located in a region that today is part of Turkey and was the epicenter of key trade routes and thus, an important center of culture and commerce. Through Paul's ministry, Ephesus also became a center of evangelism to the rest of the province of Asia, which is why Paul sojourned in the region and kept close ties with the assemblies established in that area.

In the later years of his ministry, while Paul was placed on house arrest in Rome, he penned several letters including his general epistle to the assemblies in Ephesus. This letter to the Ephesians is highlighted by his profound assessment of the spiritual battle that we face, and one for which we must possess the internal fortitude to stand in the face of opposition. Paul warns against self-reliance which is the antithesis of faith. Our key to victory is reliance on the Lord's mighty power (see Eph. 6:10). Paul also admonishes us to prepare for battle by putting on the whole armor of God, for when properly armed, we are able to withstand the strategies and tricks of satan.

Paul understood what was required to remain faithful. Despite his imprisonment, he didn't become discouraged in his faith, and his example encouraged others to endure challenging circumstances. Paul's letter to the Ephesians underscored the fact that our faith in God is personal in nature. No one or no thing can take what God has promised you. Your inheritance is secure as long as you remain faithful. However, you can forfeit God's promises if you stray from your commitment to Him. The strategies of the enemy are designed to discourage you. You must have faith that God has adequately armed you for every battle you will face. The battle is not yours; it is the Lord's, and He's already won. That means that you'll win also if you don't give up.

GONE FISHIN'

So Jesus said to them, "Children, you do not have any fish, do you?" They answered Him, "No." And He said to them, "Cast the net on the right-hand side of the boat and you will find a catch." So they cast, and then they were not able to haul it in because of the great number of fish (John 21:5-6 NASB).

One of Jesus' final appearances, after His resurrection, took place near the Sea of Galilee. On this occasion, Peter had decided to go fishing, and six of the disciples accompanied him. (Recall that several disciples were commercial fisherman when they were first recruited by Jesus.) At this time, the disciples were struggling to understand the events that had recently transpired. Although Jesus had risen from the grave, they were still apprehensive about their future. Jesus had charged them to preach the Gospel of His Kingdom, but that commission seemed far from their minds. Of particular concern was Peter's mental state. His denial of Jesus prior to the crucifixion had mired him in an internal battle with guilt and shame, and he had lost the passion he once had for ministry. His decision to go fishing was analogous to waving the white flag of surrender. During this difficult time, Peter retreated to his previous occupation and a place where he felt comfortable.

As the leader among the disciples, Peter had been very outspoken about his faith. In fact, Jesus had often warned him about his impulsive behavior and his false confidence. His subsequent denial of Jesus affected him deeply and undoubtedly caused him to question his own faith. Like many of us, Peter failed to see his weaknesses, which tests and trials will expose. Yet God stands ready to strengthen us in the areas where we are weak if we allow Him. Jesus loved Peter deeply and knew the potential he possessed. Peter really needed encouragement because he was on the verge of giving up.

Have you ever felt like giving up during a trying time in your life? Do you feel that way presently? Maybe you feel like you've failed God. Maybe you feel that God has failed you. You want to move forward, but it seems easier to revert back to your old ways. It's not that you don't love God. It's not that you don't think His Word is true. You may simply be overwhelmed by grief, shame, or disappointment. Whatever the case, you feel like giving up.

Although Peter and his fellow disciples toiled all night, they came up with nothing. And so, tired and exhausted, they prepared to head back to shore. Just as the sun rose, the disciples happened to see a man standing on the beach. Not realizing it was Jesus, they heard him ask if they had caught any fish, to which they replied no. He then instructed them to move their net to the right side of the boat and assured them that upon doing so, they would catch plenty of fish. The disciples followed His instructions, and Jesus miraculously led them to a sizeable catch. In fact, their net contained so many fish that the disciples had great difficulty drawing it in.

You may recall from Chapter 5 that Peter and several others present had a similar experience on a previous occasion—the day Jesus called them to ministry. Even so, Peter was still unaware of the identity of their friendly guide. Indeed, John had to inform Peter that the man was none other than Jesus. Upon hearing this news, Peter was so overjoyed that he jumped out of the boat and swam to shore to meet Him, while the other disciples stayed with the boat and brought the net to shore. When the other disciples arrived, Jesus had a fire burning and had prepared a meal, enabling the disciples to fellowship with Him once again.

For the second time in Scripture, we find the disciples on a fishing expedition that initially yielded no return. In some respects, it is a metaphor depicting life without Jesus. Life without Jesus is vain or empty. Sure, there may be a lot of activity, but not that which is fulfilling. This is particularly true once you've known the fullness of His love and the riches of His grace. You can't turn back because nothing compares to the abundant life that we have in Him. The circumstances of life may cause us to temporarily lose our eternal focus; however, we must always seek direction from God to ensure that we are fishing in the right pond.

Peter had reached his breaking point. Maybe you've been there too. When you arrive at this point, you have but two choices. You can either give up or you can give in. God wants you to give in. He wants to relieve you of the burdens that you needlessly carry. Jesus encourages you to bring your heavy burdens to Him so that you may be relieved (see Matt. 11:28), and at the same time, He fully prepares you for any assignment He gives you. As such, He describes His yoke as easy and light. This is in stark contrast to the burdens we often assume ourselves. Peter was carrying a self-imposed burden that Jesus had come to relieve.

On the shore, Jesus asked Peter three times if he loved Him. Each time that Peter answered affirmatively, Jesus followed with the instruction to feed His sheep. Jesus wanted Peter to understand that His love for him as well as His plan for his life had not changed. Jesus knew that once Peter had fully surrendered his will, he would not fail to carry out His commission. However, God's will had to take precedence over everything else in Peter's life. Jesus desired that Peter exchange the burden of guilt and disappointment for the privilege of preaching and teaching the Gospel.

The Test of a Man

Peter's ordeal began the night Jesus was betrayed. As Jesus shared the Passover meal with His disciples, they started to argue over who among them would be considered the greatest. (And this wasn't the first time the disciples had argued over this issue.) The timing of this dispute is curious given the grave nature of the situation. It is also interesting to note that the argument took place shortly after Jesus' tremendous act of humility—He had washed each of the disciples' feet. This task normally fell to the lowest ranking servant of a household; nevertheless, Jesus carefully washed the disciples' feet before supper.

His earlier teachings on humility as well as His demonstration earlier in the evening were obviously overlooked by the disciples. Thus, Jesus took the opportunity to correct their misguided understanding of greatness. Like many of us, the disciples had embraced a worldly perspective of greatness, but Jesus explained that true greatness was achieved through service to others and not the misuse of authority. Jesus then directed His attention to Peter, who had likely been the most vocal of the disciples and probably played a chief role in the dispute.

Jesus gave Peter a surprising revelation. Even though Peter was unwittingly about to enter a difficult period of testing, His pride would prevent him from accepting Jesus' warning. In fact, his pride was in large part the reason for his test. Jesus warned Peter that he would turn his back on Him in the immediate future. The events that Jesus foreshadowed would cause him to falter and question his faith. Knowing what was in store, Jesus informed Peter that He'd personally prayed for him. He first prayed that Peter's faith would enable him to recover from his transgression, and then He prayed that Peter would mature into an effective leader and strengthen his fellow disciples.

Like each of us, Peter had flaws. Nevertheless, Peter was a born leader, and God had a great plan for his life. Peter's destiny was to play a vital role in the spreading of the Gospel and the establishment of the Church. It should be no wonder that Peter encountered resistance. Peter was called to help perpetuate the ministry of Christ. Jesus had regularly encountered resistance because of His stand for righteousness, and it was now time for Peter and the other disciples to stand in faith. We must be stress-tested if we're going to hold up under life's pressures.

God allows us to be tested so that His character is produced in us. Peter was a prideful man. His true test was not whether he'd stumble, but rather how he'd recover after he stumbled. Peter's experience brought him to a place where he felt like giving up. Not able to continue in his own strength, Peter became acutely aware of how much he truly needed God. This is why Peter could later write that we must humble ourselves under the mighty hand of God and be exalted in His time (see 1 Pet. 5:6). Peter learned humility during this season of testing, which made him a better leader and encouraged him to turn to God during tough times. Countless people have been blessed through Peter's life because he didn't give up.

HOLD ON

We all face difficult circumstances and at one time or another have felt like giving up. When I speak of giving up, I am not necessarily referring to salvation. You may have given up on a dream that God has placed in your heart. You may have given up on a right or a privilege you are entitled to as an heir of the King. You may have given up on a relationship that God wants to mend. You may have given up on a soul who God wants to save. When you feel like giving up, take courage in knowing that God can give you the strength to hold on.

In his poem entitled "If," Rudyard Kipling makes a profound statement that epitomizes faith. Kipling speaks of forcing your heart, nerve (mind), and sinew (body) to hold on when you feel as though you can't. He states that at these times you feel as if you have nothing except your will which says to you: "Hold on!" Faith gives us access to the supernatural strength of God's Spirit. It is this strength that enables us to hold on when we feel like giving up. This is the strength of Job, the strength of Stephen, and the strength of Jesus. This is the strength that you and I have access to through faith.

We began this chapter by discussing the armor of God, a vital component being the shield of faith. It is our faith that deflects every assault of the enemy. It is our faith that protects us in every battle. When you feel like giving up, draw strength from the reservoir of living water that is the Holy Spirit. Standing in faith means that after we've gone as far as our ability will take us, God can carry us the rest of the way. Having done all you can to stand through your natural ability, God will lend you His strength if you rely on Him. I pray your strength in the Lord as you stand firmly in the power of His might.

PART V
TIME FOR ACTION

TIME FOR ACTION

But wilt thou know, O vain man, that faith without works is dead?
(James 2:20 KJV).

James, the brother of Jesus, is believed to be the author of the first general epistle that was written to the early Church. The Book of James, as it is commonly called, was written around A.D. 45 James' pragmatic approach to faith is very evident in his letter where he establishes that there are both privileges and responsibilities that come as a result of our relationship with God. The most pervasive argument in James' letter is that true faith must be expressed through action.

James describes certain of his readers as vain as he asks this poignant question: Do you recognize that faith without works is useless? I'd read this passage many times in my life, and I'd heard it quoted in many sermons. Then one day, I realized that the vain man whom James was speaking to was me. It was not written specifically to me; however, the Holy Spirit used these words to reveal certain weaknesses in my understanding of faith. "Vain," as it is used in this context, means empty or without spiritual wealth. Although I had knowledge of God's Word, I wasn't regularly producing the fruit of faith, because I didn't understand the true purpose of faith. I understood that faith often resulted in action on God's part. Nevertheless, I needed a clearer perspective of what faith demanded on my part.

James observed that our actions or good works are evidences of faith. God commands us to serve Him and to serve others. It can easily be said that faith that does not produce obedience is not faith at all. Those who love God keep His commandments. Man is God's agent for change in the earth. However, His will comes to pass only when we act in faith. While most believe faith is demonstrated through great exploits or miracles, this is not necessarily the case. God is no doubt a miracle worker; however, I've come to realize that faith is a battle of inches. Namely, it is the battle for the small space between my ears. Each decision that I make should be governed by God's Word. This is the definition of living by faith. When I adopt this attitude, God can regularly use me to accomplish things great and small.

For much of my life my perspective of faith was both limited and misguided. I was focused on my agenda in life, and faith was my means to get God to make it come to pass. I wanted God to change the world around me through my faith, whereas God simply needed to change the heart within me. Something amazing happens when you truly give your heart to God. This goes beyond religion or deliverance. I'm talking about when you reach the point where you go from being self-centered to God-centered. God can do miraculous things through your life when your heart is in tune with His and He knows that He will be glorified.

It's interesting to note that when James discussed the things that faith produces, He didn't discuss signs or wonders. While James certainly believed in miracles, having personally observed many in His own life, I believe he understood that it is easy to get sidetracked by these things. Even Jesus Himself said that signs and wonders were to persuade unbelievers. The believer is charged with the routine, but essential, work of changing him or herself. The greatest miracle you will ever experience is the transformation of your own life. This is why the action that James speaks of relates to abiding by God's Word and sharing His love. It takes most of us a while to realize that it takes faith to think, speak, and act like God. And when we think, speak, and act like God, amazing things naturally happen around us.

Earlier in my life I placed unfounded expectations on God, and at the same time, I failed to address a basic question. What does God expect of me? As I've matured, I've learned that faith means seeking God's will and doing what He requires of me. If I obey His Word, God is never slack concerning His promises. As my level of trust has grown, I actually ask God for fewer things. It's not that I don't need things. I just have the confidence that He will provide them. I speak with more confidence concerning what God can and will do on my behalf because I have come to know Him personally. By that I mean that I have learned to seek God for myself. God can and does speak to me. I also have learned to apply His Word even in difficult circumstances. This practical experience has taught me that God will act in my best interest. And though I don't get it right all the time, I've learned to trust Him more.

Faith has enabled God's Spirit to change my heart. He has healed emotional scars. He has changed unhealthy thoughts and attitudes. He has removed unrighteous desires and corrected bad habits. Faith in God has done for me what I could not do for myself. In my estimation, that is nothing less than a miracle. It is true that God will heal you of physical diseases. It is also true that God will cause you to prosper. It is true that God will exalt you before men. And it is true that God will use you to supernaturally touch the lives of others. However, the faith that God has given you is just that. It is for you! It is for you to trust God to the point that the miracle of change is affected in your life. I pray this final section of the book exhorts you to act on what you believe so that you are completely transformed into the image of His Son.

CHAPTER 13

MAKE A CHANGE

Your attitude should be the same that Christ Jesus had. Though He was God, He did not demand and cling to His rights as God. He made Himself nothing; He took the humble position of a slave and appeared in human form. And in human form He obediently humbled Himself even further by dying a criminal's death on a cross. Because of this, God raised Him up to the heights of heaven and gave Him a name that is above every other name (Philippians 2:5-9 NLT).

To what great cause should we first apply our measure of faith? Rest assured we don't have to look very far. I am persuaded that faith is most appropriately applied to changing ourselves. Our faith is what we depend on to navigate the individual course that we all must complete. The Bible speaks of concepts such as being born again, repentance, and renewal of the mind. Each of these concepts boils down to altering the way we think or changing our attitude.

Beginning with his dramatic conversion on the road to Damascus, Paul's life epitomized change. Whether through love or adversity, God choreographed the circumstances of life to carefully mold Paul into the image and likeness of Christ. Indeed, Paul was transformed from a zealous Pharisee and persecutor of the early Church to an evangelist and apostle of Christ. Initially a prideful, self-righteous man, he became a humble teacher and servant. This extraordinary change of heart that Paul experienced is convincing evidence of the work of the Holy Spirit in the life of the believer. It was also the Holy Spirit who equipped Paul to teach, exhort, and encourage others to pursue change in their personal lives.

Paul's letter to the Philippians expressed the change in attitude that his faith had produced. Despite his many trials, he had learned that the proper attitude enabled him to endure them all.

After Paul had established the church at Philippi at the beginning of his second missionary journey, the Philippians became generous supporters of Paul's ministry and were very instrumental in the spread of the Gospel. Like a caring father, Paul encouraged the Philippians in their spiritual growth. Although his epistle to the Philippians is short, it plainly articulates the impact that our faith should have on our attitude.

Your attitude generally determines your success or failure in a given situation, and there is a direct correlation between attitude and effort. Your attitude determines the confidence that others place in you, as well as the confidence you place in others. In addition, your attitude is the filter through which you view the world around you. This is why Paul admonished the Philippians to adopt the same attitude that Christ demonstrated. Paul marveled at the humility Jesus had displayed during His earthly existence, even while Jesus walked confidently in the authority that He was given. Jesus was able to balance these distinct traits because His thinking was one with God.

KINGDOM AUTHORITY

The centurion answered and said, Lord, I am not worthy that Thou shouldest come under my roof: but speak the word only, and my servant shall be healed. For I am a man under authority, having soldiers under me: and I say to this man, Go, and he goeth; and to another, Come, and he cometh; and to my servant, Do this, and he doeth it. When Jesus heard it, He marvelled, and said to them that followed, Verily I say unto you, I have not found so great faith, no, not in Israel (Matthew 8:8-10 KJV).

When Jesus returned to Capernaum from an excursion, He was approached by several highly respected Jewish elders. An officer of the Roman army had asked these elders to entreat Jesus on his behalf regarding a highly esteemed servant who was sick and near death. The elders, in turn, earnestly pleaded with Jesus to help the centurion. This is noteworthy given the divisiveness between Jews and Gentiles during that time. This particular officer had established a good rapport among the Jews and had even built the Jews a local synagogue. Jesus was compelled by their plea and offered to go to the officer's home with the elders.

This officer happened to be a centurion, which meant that one hundred Roman soldiers were under his command. In addition to his position in the military, he also had servants who worked in his household. Considering his important position in the Roman army and his respected social status, he still expressed great humility toward Jesus. For when the officer received word that Jesus was on His way, he sent messengers to meet Him. This officer did not consider himself worthy enough that Jesus should come to his house, nor did he consider himself worthy enough to come to Jesus in person. Instead, he instructed the messengers to speak with Jesus regarding his servant.

Note that the officer had developed a great appreciation for authority. He was subject to the authority of superior officers and responsible for many subordinates; and whenever he gave a command, his instructions were dutifully carried out. The officer recognized Jesus as a man of unequaled authority, and he perceived that Jesus could command things to occur supernaturally. He believed that if Jesus simply gave the order, his servant would be healed.

Jesus marveled at this man's faith, and He was so impressed by it that He testified to the crowd who followed Him. Jesus claimed He'd never witnessed such faith, not even among the nation of Israel. The officer understood the authority that Jesus was given and placed his trust in Him. While the officer was not a Jew or even religious for that matter, he still possessed something that many of the Jews lacked—he had a Kingdom mentality. He readily accepted and submitted to Jesus' authority. This kind of faith distinguished him from most of his contemporaries, Jews and Gentiles alike. Jesus could have just as easily declared that He'd never met anyone with his type of attitude; but it was this man's faith that caused him to think differently, and it was this way of thinking that pleasantly surprised Jesus. First, we observe the officer's humility. He afforded Jesus the respect that is due a king. Second, we observe his selflessness. He clearly cared for his servant's welfare and went to great lengths to ensure his recovery. Finally, we observe his confidence. He expressed a ridiculous level of faith that elicited high praise from Jesus Himself.

The officer's response to his servant's sickness was uncommon. Most people given similar circumstances would have thrown in the towel. Not the officer. Faced with a situation that was beyond his natural abilities, the officer sought a higher authority. We must remember that God is the ultimate authority and His ruling will prevail. The surest way to influence the outcome of a situation is to take your plea to the highest authority. However, you will not act in this manner unless you allow God to change your attitude through faith.

The officer's story is important because it demonstrates that God's power is not accessed through religious ritual or protocol. The heart of God is moved by faith, pure and simple. When we condition ourselves to think like Him, He has an open door into our affairs. The officer demonstrated the mind of Christ. As a result, Jesus gave the order for his servant to be healed. The Bible records that the servant was healed in that very hour. This account demonstrates the awesome possibilities when we adopt a Christ-like attitude.

A Royal Perspective

When Jesus walked the earth, He preached a recurring message: The Kingdom from Heaven has arrived! This message implies that Christ is King and has restored mankind as the rightful authority in the earth. The Roman officer understood what it meant to think like a king. His actions underscored the truth that the Kingdom from

Heaven had arrived and Christ was indeed the King. Likewise, we must mature to the extent that we exhibit the same type of faith. God is always in control of your circumstances, regardless of how things may appear. So, if you are going to walk in faith, you must first see the world from His perspective.

Jesus came to give sight to the blind. In turn, that is exactly what the Word of God does. It opens our spiritual eyes. Consider the story of Jesus meeting with Nicodemus at night. He told Nicodemus that he had to be born again in order to understand the Kingdom of Heaven. The term "born again" refers to the way we think. In essence, Jesus was saying that in order to walk in the authority that He has ordained for us, we must reject our worldly view and adopt His heavenly view. However, we can achieve this only if we acquire the knowledge of His Word and the revelation of His Spirit.

If you want to see the world from God's vantage point, you must allow Him to move you to higher ground. You must never allow yourself to be mired in the base things of life, and you must make complacency your enemy. As Paul admonishes, you must press toward the mark of your high calling in Christ (see Phil. 3:14), pressing onward and upward toward the place where Jesus is. As you ascend, you will see the world around you more clearly with God's Word guiding you along the way. His Spirit will lead you to the mountain to enjoy a heavenly view.

In describing His vantage point, God said it is not to be compared. God declares that He sees the end from the beginning (see Isa. 46:10). Hence, God's thoughts are beyond our limited thinking. People and circumstances look quite different when we view them from God's perspective; God is always looking toward destiny and is not preoccupied with temporal things or conditions. It's not always easy for us to see things from God's vantage point, because we often focus on the wrong things. Therefore, we must lay aside any distraction and sin because these impede our climb. Faith compels us to continue our ascension in life because we gradually see things from God's perspective.

A NEW ATTITUDE

Earlier in this chapter we discussed the centurion and his Kingdom mentality. Interestingly enough, Jesus had difficulty instilling this type of attitude in His own disciples. The disciples, like many of us, were well-intentioned; however, Jesus had to constantly correct their understanding and challenge their thinking. Their culture, religion, environment, and experiences greatly affected their attitude. Jesus worked tirelessly to become the dominant influence in their lives, and He expected His words to guide their decisions.

One day, the disciples came to Jesus inquiring who among them was the greatest, a recurring debate among the group. Again, their question revealed their limited understanding of His Kingdom. Their view of Christ's Kingdom was no different from their view of the world's kingdoms where worldly rulers commonly forced their will upon others. This would not be the case in Christ's Kingdom, however. Those who desired to rule would earn that right only through humble service. Jesus provided a poignant example to demonstrate this truth.

As Jesus summoned a small child nearby and set him in the midst of the disciples, He told them that their attitude should resemble that of the small child, otherwise they would not understand or enter His Kingdom. Jesus further explained that humility was the key to greatness in His Kingdom. Jesus often spoke of the reward of humility. He said that the humble would be exalted and that the meek would inherit His Kingdom. The lower you go, the higher He will take you. The disciples struggled to understand this concept because they hadn't been converted. Although they were followers of Christ, they hadn't yet adopted His mentality. As a result, they had good intentions, but bad attitudes. Recall that your attitude is the way you see yourself and the world around you.

What was true of the disciples is largely true of many of us today. We often have good intentions, but don't have the proper attitude. Like the disciples, we require circumcision of the heart in order to correct our vision. Church attendance or religious activity does not equate to conversion, and accepting Jesus as Lord and Savior is but our first step for entry to Christ's Kingdom.

The Kingdom is an invisible reality. This is why Jesus told a group of misguided religious leaders that His Kingdom would not come with visible signs (see Luke 17:20). In our present lives we see and experience God's Kingdom only through faith, so we must allow God to change our attitude if we are to understand the principles by which His Kingdom operates.

Someone once told me that people change, but not much—the implication being that change is often difficult. And we often find it difficult to change because of our attitude. In fact, it is impossible to rise above your attitude. I have come to understand that faith is essential for change in the human heart. And in order to change, you must see things differently. Most importantly, you must see yourself the way God sees you. The Bible affirms that through Christ we can be made new creatures (see 2 Cor. 5:17). In other words, Christ gives us the power to change, and we are no longer slaves to our past hurts, addictions, tendencies, or emotions.

When we look from our perspective, it is easy to believe that we cannot change. This is why God has to change our perspective. We must digest a steady diet of God's Word so that it becomes a part of our spiritual DNA. In this way, our perspective is transformed from the inside out. This is what Paul meant when he remarked that we are transformed by the renewing of our minds. Christ does not offer a temporary fix. Instead, we are completely and permanently changed. The Bible speaks of this glorious change when it affirms that we are presently the sons of God. Though we can't see it visibly, the transformation is taking place on the inside. God has given you the power to change the world, but the change must first be affected inside of you.

CHAPTER 14

ASK IN PRAYER

Confess your faults one to another, and pray one for another, that ye may be healed. The effectual fervent prayer of a righteous man availeth much (James 5:16 KJV).

James was a great laborer in the Gospel and even presided over the assembly at Jerusalem. In so doing, he helped establish many early believers in their faith, which is exemplified in the paternal tone of his letter. In this epistle, he focuses on many practical disciplines of the believer's life, providing sensible prescriptions for maturing in faith. His letter also addresses fundamental aspects of faith such as enduring temptation, sacrificial giving, and careful speech. James' traditional Jewish upbringing also influenced his perspective of faith and his leadership of the Church.

James' disciplined approach to faith was very evident by his lifestyle. He was surnamed "the Just" because of his strong character and chaste behavior. James placed particular emphasis on prayer, and tradition says that he was also referred to as "Old Camel Knees" because of the amount of time he spent in prayer. His epistle certainly depicts a man who valued time spent in prayer. Moreover, the letter of James gives us the proper perspective of prayer. He admonished his fellow believers that effective prayer, prayer that has power, required a consecrated lifestyle. It should not surprise his readers that James ends his letter with an emphasis on prayer, as well.

The objective of his letter is to instruct and exhort believers who are experiencing problems, while the appeal of James' letter is the practicality and simplicity with which he addresses the basic challenges that we encounter as we endeavor to exercise faith. After providing clear instruction and practical wisdom, James concludes with the remedy that was most familiar and most reliable in his experience. James knew through experience that prayer changes things. He observed that there was a powerful link between prayer and faith. As such, he could personally attest that the effectual, fervent prayers of righteous individuals produce results.

ASK IN PRAYER

Jesus answered and said unto them, Verily I say unto you, If ye have faith, and doubt not, ye shall not only do this which is done to the fig tree, but also if ye shall say unto this mountain, Be thou removed, and be thou cast into the sea; it shall be done. And all things, whatsoever ye shall ask in prayer, believing, ye shall receive (Matthew 21:21-22 KJV).

During the final days of His ministry, Jesus traveled with His disciples between Bethany and Jerusalem, and as they journeyed, Jesus noticed a fig tree in the distance. Being hungry, He went closer to the tree to find out if there was fruit on it. While fig trees produce crops, for the most part, in the fall, they also yield a small edible fruit in the spring, which Jesus may have expected to find during this springtime season. Yet when Jesus reached the tree, He realized that there was no fruit available. He then cursed the tree, declaring that it would never bear fruit again. His disciples continued on their way, giving little thought to this insignificant occurrence.

The next day, as the disciples traveled along the same path, they observed the same fig tree—this time withered up from the roots. Peter then remembered Jesus' statement and marveled that the fig tree had died in response to His judgment. The other disciples were also amazed and were eager to understand how the fig tree withered so quickly. Jesus told the disciples that if they had faith, they, too, could exercise authority over the fig tree. Even more, they could tell a mountain, "Go throw yourself in the sea," and it would happen. Jesus promised the disciples that if they believed, they would receive whatever they asked for in prayer.

At first blush the reference to prayer is a curious one. The event in question does not appear to involve prayer. However, we must consider our perspective of prayer. Prayer involves agreement or coming together. Prayer is not limited by time, place, or conditions. While we may have preferred circumstances, we always have the ability to commune with God. Hebrew definitions for prayer include intervention, mediation, and judgment. When Jesus spoke to the fig tree, He judged it, or, thought of another way, He prayed. Jesus had a right to pronounce judgment over the tree because of His authority in the earth. Jesus also regularly communed with God prior to the beginning of the day, whereas we tend to pray when opportunities or problems arise. Jesus was wiser and prayed *because* opportunities and problems arise. As such, He was adequately prepared for the situations He encountered each day.

Jesus used this opportunity to demonstrate to His disciples the link between prayer and faith. Our authorization to dominate the earth comes from God who is also the source of our power. Therefore, if we want Him to effect change on our behalf, we must meet Him in prayer. Prayer is the time we receive instructions and clarity regarding God's will for our lives. We do not have to consult God for everything that occurs in the earth. However, we must come into agreement with God if we expect Him to intervene. In the case of the tree, Jesus pronounced a judgment that defied the laws of nature. Nonetheless, He was simply acting based on the authorization He received in prayer.

Prayer is closely linked to faith because through prayer we develop confidence in God. Recall that faith is complete trust or reliance on another. How can we rely on God's plan for our lives if we are not aware of it? How can we uncover God's plan for our lives if we do not meet Him in prayer? It is also important to note that Jesus' promise to His disciples was specific. He told the disciples that they could have whatever they asked for *in prayer*. Note that He did not say they could simply have whatever they requested. The stipulation was that the request be made *in prayer*—or in agreement with God. It is in prayer that we meet with God to agree on the course our lives should take. It is that plan that God authorizes and that plan that we can have faith in.

PRAYER THAT AVAILS

I imagine that most people reading this book have prayed at some point in their lives. Some may pray regularly and others may pray infrequently. It is interesting to note that one does not have to be pious or religious to pray. Prayer, believe it or not, is instinctive. There is a part of all of us that is spirit and longs to commune with God. However, prayer can be a frustrating activity if we don't fully understand the objective of prayer.

Have you ever prayed and felt as though your prayer went unanswered? Have you ever petitioned God for something that you never received? If you are like me, it's not a matter of *if* this ever happened, but how many times it *has* happened. How did you feel during these times? Angry? Despondent? Confused? Prayers that appear to be unanswered erode our faith. If we come to believe that God will not or cannot answer our prayers, we may come to question our relationship with Him or even His very existence.

If you desire to grow stronger in faith and develop a closer relationship with God, a regular prayer life is essential. However, you must have a clear understanding of prayer and its proper application. For most of my life, I assumed prayer was simply talking to God. It's interesting to note that I spent most of my prayer time asking for things. If I wasn't asking, I wasn't doing much talking. Moreover, I was doing very little listening.

In retrospect, I don't believe that I really expected God to answer. I certainly desired the things I requested, but I didn't have confidence that

I'd actually receive them. There is little in life more disheartening than an unfulfilled prayer life. I know this through personal experience. As I alluded to earlier, my breakthrough came as a result of the timeless words of James' general epistle to the Church. "Effectual, fervent prayer greatly avails." This simple yet profound statement unlocks the door to a rewarding prayer life.

THREE QUALIFICATIONS FOR MEETING WITH GOD

If we examine James' statement closely, we note three qualifications for prayer or communion with God. The objective of prayer is the first qualification that James mentions. *Effectual* means to work as intended. I realized I did not have a proper understanding of prayer. As I stated before, I thought prayer simply involved talking to God. Upon further investigation, I learned that prayer was much more. Prayer actually means to come together or to bring into agreement. It involves communion with God and not simply communication. For prayer to work as intended, we must learn God's plan for our lives and bring our thoughts, words, and actions into agreement. Prayer is not simply a time to log requests. It is a one-on-one meeting with the God of creation.

The second qualification speaks to the way that we pray. James says that prayer should be fervent or earnest. Many people often confuse earnestness with emotion. God knows the true condition of our hearts and is not moved by emotionalism per se. He is however moved by those who have a true zeal for seeking His will. We must be committed to prayer. This occurs only when we understand the purpose and the vital importance of prayer.

The third qualification speaks to our relationship with God. A righteous individual is one who enjoys a covenant relationship with God. It is akin to a bond such as marriage. When we have the proper relationship with God, He is responsible for our well-being. God has a standing offer to anyone who desires this relationship, and it begins by accepting Him as Lord. He commits to leading us and providing for us. In turn, we commit to serving Him by living according to His Word. When this type of relationship exists, God readily meets us in prayer.

THREE KEYS TO ANSWERED PRAYER

We noted earlier that prayer can be a frustrating activity. Unanswered prayer erodes our faith. Thus, it is important to understand the symbiotic relationship between prayer and faith. Prayer strengthens your faith, and faith manifests your prayer. Through prayer you uncover God's plan for your life and give Him permission to involve Himself in your affairs. While I am sure others may have their own recipe, I have uncovered three keys that lead to answered prayer, and each key corresponds to the qualifications previously outlined.

Regarding effectual prayer, we discussed that for prayer to work as intended we must come into agreement with God. In the same general epistle referenced earlier, James cautions fellow believers about asking amiss (see James 4:3). He tells them that the reason they don't receive many of the things they ask for is that their motivations are self-centered. In essence, James tells his readers that many of the things they ask for are outside of God's will for their lives. The first key to answered prayer is praying according to the Word of God. God's Word is full of principles and promises that are sure. (The next chapter examines this truth more closely.) When you pray according to God's Word, you demonstrate your reverence of Him and your acceptance of His plan for your life. This attitude draws you close to the heart of God and is generally rewarded by answered prayer.

The Word of God also admonishes us to pray under the leading of the Holy Spirit. Our covenant relationship with God establishes the most intimate relationship possible—His Spirit literally lives on the inside of us. The Holy Spirit prepares us to listen and receive instructions regarding God's will for our lives so that we know what to request. What's more, the Spirit will pray for us if we yield ourselves. Many people are fearful of the idea of praying in the Spirit or an unknown tongue because they do not understand that it is the Spirit of God interceding for them. This, too, requires an act of faith, trusting that if He said it in His Word, it will work for your benefit.

The second qualification we noted earlier was fervency—that we must be committed and earnest concerning prayer. Certain things in life are simple but not necessarily easy. Prayer definitely falls into this category. The second key to answered prayer is simply consistency. Consistency is something I have often struggled with in my prayer life. So I must regularly remind myself of Paul's admonishment to the Thessalonians to pray without ceasing (see 1 Thess. 5:17). Recall that prayer is an appointment with God. How can we expect God to do anything in our lives if we will not meet with Him regularly? When we fail to meet with God in prayer, it is tantamount to saying that we don't require His assistance. Conversely, a consistent prayer life results in an intimate relationship with God and regular answers to our prayers. This does not imply that God answers how and when we want. However, it does mean that if we faithfully seek Him, He will be there to meet us and He won't fail to answer us.

The final qualification we discussed is righteousness. James clearly noted that the prayers of righteous people greatly avail. Consequently, the final key to answered prayer is righteous living. Righteousness is not something we earn. It is credited to us when we express a sincere desire to do God's will and follow that expression with effort. Because God is holy, we have to live holy if we want to maintain a relationship with Him. Living holy requires us to dedicate ourselves to God. His will must supercede our own. Living holy does not mean we will not make mistakes. The Bible says that all have sinned and fall short of God's glory (see Rom. 3:23). However, holiness does require that we make every effort to live according to His Word. It also requires us to change when we find ourselves in error. God will faithfully meet you in prayer as long as you continue to strive to do His will.

HOW DID JESUS PRAY?

Earlier in this chapter we examined the relationship between prayer and faith, and we observed that effective prayer builds our relationship with God and our confidence in His Word. Prayer is essential to the welfare of our inner man, and Jesus' life on earth was a testament to this truth. Prayer is prevalent throughout the accounts of Jesus' time in the earth. In addition to regular devotional time, we find that Jesus prayed prior to important decisions as well as during stressful times.

Jesus clearly demonstrated the necessity of prayer. He also regularly admonished His disciples regarding their prayer lives and instructed them to constantly pray (see Luke 18:1). At times, He used illustrations to demonstrate the importance of fervency and humility in prayer. The disciples recognized the frequent nature of Jesus' admonishments, and they associated His strength of character with His devoted prayer life. Upon a return from a regular devotion, one of the disciples asked Jesus to teach them to pray effectively (see Luke 11:1). It was at this point that Jesus provided His disciples with a well-documented model for prayer.

The model Jesus provided is actually pretty straightforward. He began by telling His disciples to honor or acknowledge God. Recall that honor or praise ushers us into the presence of God. We must enter God's presence in order for us to ask *in prayer*. Secondly, Jesus told His disciples to pray for the manifestation of God's Kingdom and for His will to be carried out in the earth. Our trust in God is demonstrated by subjecting our will to His will. In a spiritual sense, we are waving the white flag of surrender and giving God the right to work in and through our lives. We also affirm our hope in the manifestation of His eternal Kingdom in the fullness of time.

The third step in the model actually involves serving God. Jesus instructed the disciples to ask God to afford them necessary provisions day by day. In essence, Jesus was telling them to trust God to supply them with what they needed inasmuch as they had committed their lives to service for Him. We often pray for all types of things that we want as opposed to simply asking God to supply what we need. I believe in this respect we often pray amiss. God is able to do exceeding abundantly above all we can ask or think (see Eph. 3:20); we simply have to trust Him enough to afford Him the opportunity to deliver on that promise.

The fourth step in the model requires believers to ask for forgiveness. We must be in right standing with God for our prayers to avail. God imputes righteousness to us; however, we must ask forgiveness if we are aware we have sinned. We qualify for God's forgiveness by forgiving others who may have done us wrong. Finally, Jesus instructed His disciples to pray for the strength to overcome temptation. Jesus warned them on many occasions that they must endure temptation. As He was fond of saying, the servant is not above his master. In that respect, we all will be tempted just as Jesus was tempted. His desire is that the Spirit strengthens us through His Word when we are tempted.

We previously examined Jesus' prayer in the Garden of Gethsemane, where He said, "Thy will be done." This prayer is unquestionably the most pivotal prayer in the history of mankind. Jesus' victory over sin and death restored mankind as God's authority in the earth, and this momentous accomplishment is directly linked to His prayer on that fateful night. Moreover, it is linked to His lifelong commitment to prayer. Jesus could have elected a different course of action; however, He understood that the ultimate purpose of prayer is that God's will be done in the earth. God has impregnated each of us, like Jesus, with the potential to make an indelible mark on the present world. In part, we unleash our potential by committing to a life of prayer.

CHAPTER 15

SPEAK THE WORD

It is written: "I believed; therefore I have spoken." With that same spirit of faith we also believe and therefore speak (2 Corinthians 4:13 NIV).

Earlier in this text we referenced Paul's second letter to the assembly of believers at Corinth. Paul wrote, in part, about the immeasurable value of God's Word and described it as precious treasure stored within us. Paul understood the dynamic power of God's Word and its ability to transform our lives and the world around us. Though we may find ourselves distressed, confused, or persecuted, God's Word has the power to keep us. Moreover, our faith in God's Word produces an eternal glory that is greater than anything we can imagine (see 2 Cor. 4:17). God's Word is the basis for His relationship with mankind. It reveals His will concerning us, orders the natural world in which we live, and holds the keys to His eternal Kingdom. If we aspire to truly walk in faith, God's Word should govern the things we say.

When you enjoy a covenant relationship with God, you are entitled to the promises in His Word. Nevertheless, knowing your rights is not enough. Recall that belief is our conviction in God's ability to perform His Word, and faith involves acting on our conviction or belief. While faith is synonymous with action, it often begins and ends with the words we speak. In his second letter to the Corinthians, Paul quotes the Psalmist who wrote, "I have believed therefore have spoken" (see Ps. 116:10). Your confession is born out of your conviction. This is to say that what you believe determines what you say and not the other way around.

Jesus noted that our spoken words reveal what is in our heart (see Luke 6:45). That's why you must store God's Word in your heart. To act in faith you must first have knowledge of God's Word; then you must accept the Word and rely on it. When you store God's Word in your heart, it naturally influences what you say. Confession is an essential step toward walking in faith because it brings you into agreement with God. After all, do two men walk together unless they agree to do so? (see Amos 3:3).

Confession in this context does not simply refer to an admission of sin or guilt. Confession is a declaration of truth inspired by a commitment to do God's will. When you understand the true meaning of confession, you realize that your words should never be influenced by external circumstances. God's Word is stored in your heart so that you can speak what God has declared concerning you. You demonstrate your faith in God by confessing what His Word says about a situation rather than confessing how a situation appears. When you declare God's Word, God responds because He is one with His Word.

Far too often we allow our emotions to influence what we say. When we speak contrary to God's Word, we demonstrate a lack of knowledge or a lack of faith; therefore we must search God's Word to learn His will concerning situations we encounter. When challenges or trials present themselves, we must stand firm on the Word that we have stored in our heart. Whenever God wants to effect change in the earth, He simply speaks. Therefore, if you want the power of God to cause change in your life, you must allow God to speak to you concerning your situation. Having heard from God, you can boldly declare the Word He has imparted to you.

THE CALM AFTER THE STORM

And He arose, and rebuked the wind, and said unto the sea, Peace, be still. And the wind ceased, and there was a great calm. And He said unto them, Why are ye so fearful? how is it that ye have no faith? And they feared exceedingly, and said one to another, What manner of man is this, that even the wind and the sea obey Him? (Mark 4:39-41 KJV).

It was evening and Jesus had just completed another busy day of ministry. Now He was instructing His disciples to enter their boat in order to cross over to the eastern shore of the Sea of Galilee. Although this body of water is only eight miles wide, it is located in an unpredictable climate. The lake is approximately 700 feet below sea level and surrounded by mountains on three sides. The chilly mountain air and the warm conditions near the lake create volatile weather patterns. Even today it is not uncommon for sudden storms to occur during evening hours.

Jesus was likely exhausted after the long day and apparently went to sleep shortly after they began their trip across the lake. As a windstorm suddenly arose, the resulting turbulence caused great waves to buffet their small ship, and the situation quickly became life-threatening with the boat taking on water. Fearful for their safety, the disciples frantically woke Jesus who was still sleeping in the stern of the boat—something the disciples could not understand. They wondered aloud how He could sleep through such volatile conditions and if He understood the precarious nature of their situation. Jesus did not initially respond to the disciples' question but simply turned to the matter at hand by rebuking the wind and commanding it simply to be still. In an instant, the wind became perfectly calm and the storm dissipated almost as suddenly as it had formed.

Jesus then turned His attention to His disciples with a familiar question. How is it that you have so little faith? The disciples did not yet fully understand the authority that Jesus walked in. When He instructed them to go over to the other side, He had every intention of making sure they arrived safely—the promise was implicit in His instruction. The fact that Jesus was asleep during the storm was indicative of His state of mind. Jesus was fully confident that He would arrive at His destination in spite of any unexpected weather. Likewise, we must have confidence that God will see us safely along the road that He leads us.

As the disciples reflected on what had occurred, they were filled with awe and talked among themselves about the great miracle they had just witnessed. "Who is this man, that even the sea and wind obey Him?" Jesus walked in such authority that when He spoke, the laws of nature obeyed Him. While it is unlikely that we will command the forces of nature, our words do affect the physical and spiritual worlds around us.

God has charged mankind to represent Him in the earth, and the surest way to influence the outcome of a situation is to declare His will concerning the situation. It was God's will that the disciples make it to the other side of the lake safely. Therefore, Jesus commanded the wind to be still and grant them free passage. As we've noted before, God's Word reveals His will concerning our lives. When we speak God's Word, we enter into a verbal contract with Him—a contract that He stands ready, willing, and able to fulfill.

When God wanted to restore man as His authority in the earth, He sent His Word—Jesus. The Word of God literally stepped into our reality, taking on the form of a man. Jesus revealed God's nature and our true nature. When He was in the world, He walked in sovereign authority; natural elements and spiritual beings alike obeyed Him. He demonstrated that God's Word is law and governs the world around us. If we accept this truth, we can more readily exercise faith. And when we speak His Word, He calms the storms in our life and causes miraculous things to happen.

THE LIVING WORD

In order to grasp the importance of speaking the Word, we must understand how God communicates. God can and does use various vessels to communicate to us. God may communicate through a messenger, the written Word, or His Spirit. The style of communication may be audible, or it may simply be an inward knowing. Whoever the vessel and whatever the method, it is vital to know that it is always the Word of God that is speaking. The Word of God was with God from the beginning, and it was through His Word that all things were created.

God's Word established the principles that frame or order the world around us (see Heb. 11:3). This is why God has provided us with His written Word. The New Testament often refers to the written Word of God. In most instances, it is translated from the Greek word *logos*, which means an expression or thought. In this respect, the Bible reveals the mind or intent of God. While it is important to recognize that in most instances the Bible is not speaking expressly to us, we learn of God's will or intent through the biblical accounts of people just like us. When we study His Word, we learn what to expect from God and what He expects of us. This becomes the basis of our trust in Him.

The New Testament also refers to the spoken word of God, which is translated from the Greek word *rhema*. This word is often associated with God's Spirit and is considered the living word. When Jesus spoke expressly to an individual or about a particular situation, this was a living word. Many individuals discount the importance of God's written Word because they don't understand the nature of God. God says that He does not change. He also says that His Word never returns void. Therefore, if God has already spoken concerning a situation, you have the ammunition you need to apply to your personal situation. When we read an account of God's promise to a believer in the Bible, we can have assurance that God extends the same privileges to us. It begins as a written Word, but if we apply it to our situations, it becomes a living word for us.

EVERY WORD COUNTS

We often take our words for granted, failing to understand the impact on our lives and the lives of others. However, God pays close attention to the words we speak. Jesus warned that we inevitably must account for every careless word we speak. He went on to note that it is by our words that we are justified or condemned (see Matt. 12:37). The takeaway here is clear. Our words greatly influence the quality of our lives. This is why our words should agree with the Word of God. Once we accept Jesus as Lord, there are only two things that can prevent His Word from bearing fruit in our lives. The first is our words, and the second is our walk. Our walk will be the focus of the following chapter, so for now we will focus on our words.

Have you ever said something that was in direct conflict with God's Word? The Word declares by Jesus' stripes we are healed, yet some of us continue to claim sickness (see 1 Pet. 2:24). God promises to supply all our needs, yet some of us complain about our lack of resources (see Phil. 4:19). The Word declares that whom the Son makes free is free indeed, and yet some of us say we can't let go of our addictions (see John 8:36). Do you get the picture? Our journey of faith is at times a paradox. We seek God fervently and at the same time lean on our own understanding. In Chapter 2 we discussed opposing worlds colliding—our present circumstances and our future reality promised by God. In many respects, the battle is to influence what you ultimately say. If your words conflict with God's Word, you annul His promises.

Careless words can disqualify you from the race before you've even started. As such, we must be careful when we speak. Words are an incredible resource. We never run out of them. However, our own words can literally come back to haunt us; because like God's words, our words do not return empty. They create real consequences in our lives. Therefore, we must allow the Spirit to guide us, and as James admonishes, we should be slow to speak (see James 1:19).

Speak Life

The Bible records many things about our tongue and subsequently the words we speak. Solomon may have spoken most profoundly when he declared the tongue has the power of life and death (see Prov. 18:21). He continued by stating that those who love it shall eat its fruit. I believe that Solomon correctly identified the power of our words. You can rightly conclude that you enhance your life or diminish it by the words you speak. Furthermore, if you use your words wisely, you will prosper by them.

The Bible also records a profound vision of Ezekiel the prophet. In the vision, Ezekiel is carried to a valley filled with human bones (see Ezek. 37:1). Here, Ezekiel observes that the bones are very dry, indicating the people had been deceased for some time. The Lord asks Ezekiel if the bones can become living people again. Surprised by the question, Ezekiel responds by telling God He alone knows the answer. God then instructs Ezekiel to speak to the dry bones. More specifically, he tells him to declare the Word of the Lord to the dry bones; it is the Lord's will that the deceased people live again. Therefore, Ezekiel declares God's will, and not his own, concerning the situation. After prophesying to the dry bones, Ezekiel watches in awe as muscle, flesh, and skin are formed on the bones. Then Ezekiel declares the Word of the Lord a second time and witnesses the bodies come back to life. Although this vision pertains to the nation of Israel, there is an important principle that is demonstrated concerning God's Word.

Metaphorically, we understand that God's Word must be applied to circumstances in our lives regardless of how things appear. Like Ezekiel, we must cultivate a relationship with God so that He will reveal His will concerning us. We are His representatives in the earth and the agents for change, and He requires that we learn, declare, and carry out His will. In addition, God's Word instills confidence in our hearts. This confidence does not come from simply knowing His Word; it results from knowing that we've heard from God. We first accept the Word we receive and accordingly speak based on what we believe.

God is so awesome that the words He declared thousands of years ago have the power to change your life today. You unleash the power of God by speaking His Word concerning your circumstances. Every time you speak His Word in faith, it is as if God speaks again. This is why one of the most vital functions of the Holy Spirit is to both teach you and remind you of God's Word (see John 14:26). Every day you have the opportunity to change your life and the lives of those around you with the words that you speak. You can inspire, admonish, restore, and even resurrect when you proclaim God's Word. God charges each of us to declare His Word to a dying world. When you speak His Word, you speak life into the world around you.

CHAPTER 16

WALK BY FAITH

For we that are in this tabernacle do groan, being burdened: not for that we would be unclothed, but clothed upon, that mortality might be swallowed up of life. Now He that hath wrought us for the selfsame thing is God, who also hath given unto us the earnest of the Spirit. Therefore we are always confident, knowing that, whilst we are at home in the body, we are absent from the Lord: (For we walk by faith, not by sight) (2 Corinthians 5:4-7 KJV).

Aside from Jesus, the apostle Paul is the most dominant character of the New Testament. He had been personally commissioned by Jesus to preach His Kingdom message to the Gentile world, and during his three missionary journeys, he established a number of local assemblies. It was during his final journey that one such assembly was founded at Corinth. The Bible records two letters that Paul wrote to the assembly at Corinth, and both letters are believed to have been written in the same year. His second letter to the Corinthians, written during a time of great physical and emotional distress, is arguably his most personal and heartfelt correspondence.

In a key stanza in his letter, Paul speaks of the challenges of daily life, and he addresses the duality of the earthly existence of every believer. Although we cherish and even cling to our present lives, we have an expectation of something far greater. It was this hope of eternal life with Christ Jesus that enabled Paul to overcome life's trials. He rightly concluded that in this life we must walk by faith and not by sight.

Paul's statement succinctly characterizes the life of the believer. In order to overcome the trials of life and ultimately live a life that pleases God, we must act on God's Word. It's not sufficient to know God's Word. It's also not sufficient to declare God's Word. Our actions must be governed by God's Word, and our confidence must be in God alone. Walking by faith is not always easy because it often requires us to reject what we see. By that I do not mean to suggest that we ignore the things around us. I simply submit that what we see is not all that is.

By definition (and design), our walk of faith involves uncertainty, whereas God's promises are sure. However, we may not have knowledge of how He will bring them to pass. For example, God promises that we will reap a harvest if we don't give up (see Gal. 6:9). While we have confidence that a harvest is in store, we don't know how long we have to wait. Therefore, we must walk by faith. We have to continue to obey God even if it is not apparent when or how the promise will be fulfilled.

WHY SWIM WHEN YOU CAN WALK?

About three o'clock in the morning Jesus came to them, walking on the water. When the disciples saw Him, they screamed in terror, thinking He was a ghost. But Jesus spoke to them at once. "It's all right," He said. "I am here! Don't be afraid." Then Peter called to Him, "Lord if it's really You, tell me to come to You by walking on water" (Matthew 14:25-28 NLT).

In Chapter 6, we discussed the miracle when Jesus fed over five thousand people with five loaves of bread and two fish, and it wouldn't be long before Jesus performed yet another miracle. Immediately after feeding the large crowd, Jesus had sent the people home. He then instructed His disciples to get into the boat and travel to the other side of the Sea of Galilee while He went into the hills alone to pray. The disciples quickly departed, expecting to meet Him on the other side.

Partway across the sea, the disciples ran into trouble. As the winds became violent, they had to fight heavy waves, and being far away from land, they knew it was too late to turn back. Then suddenly, even as they were already fearful due to the sudden change in conditions, the disciples saw a figure walking toward them on the water. I can hardly imagine their terror. There they were, being tossed about by the violent wind and waves, fighting to keep their ship afloat, and in the midst of these stormy conditions appears Jesus walking on these horrendous waves. He apparently paused some distance from the boat, instinctively knowing what would happen next. Believing Him to be a ghost, the disciples cried out in fear. Subsequently, Jesus identified Himself, encouraging them and telling them not to be afraid.

Peter, in his usual impulsive manner, quickly responded to Jesus, calling to Him and asking if he could walk to Him on the water. And Jesus commanded Peter to come. Without hesitation, Peter climbed out of the boat and began to walk to Jesus on the water. Imagine his astonishment and that of the other disciples—he was literally walking on water. Peter had mastered walking by faith...or had he? As Peter was walking, his focus started to leave Jesus and turned to the violent waves around him, and his initial childlike faith was quickly replaced by fear. As this fear crept in, Peter began to sink, causing him to cry out for Jesus to save him.

We can observe quite a bit from this account. The first thing is that Jesus quickly came to the aid of His disciples when they were in trouble. Although their situation had taken a turn for the worse, they were on an assignment from the Lord. This alone was assurance that they would make it to the other side. I believe that Jesus arrived at that point because their faith was failing. He came both to teach and encourage them. The Spirit operates the same way in our lives. It teaches us or reveals to us

God's will concerning us, and when we encounter trying circumstances, it reminds us of the truth we already know.

We also observe that if we trust God's Word, we can do the seemingly impossible. Peter asked Jesus for the ability to do the impossible, and based on a simple command, he did just that. He did not confer with the other disciples, and he didn't wait for better or safer conditions for a test run. He simply climbed out of the boat and began to walk on water. Peter was often impulsive, yet this trait made him a perfect candidate for walking on water. He essentially acted without thinking. When we are sure we've heard from God, we have to act without reservation. By this I mean that we must not allow our own intellect or experience to prevent us from obeying God's instructions. It is only when we receive the Word with childlike faith that God can freely operate in our lives.

A HELPING HAND

When Peter cried out, Jesus immediately reached out His hand and caught him. After rescuing Peter, He began to admonish him regarding his weakness of faith. Jesus asked Peter why he'd doubted Him. Note that Jesus established Himself as the object of Peter's faith. The implication was that Peter lacked confidence in God's Word. Recall that when Peter asked Jesus if he could walk to Him on the water, Jesus did not give him permission to come part of the way, rather He instructed Peter to travel the entire distance. Nevertheless, the feat required Peter to exercise faith. As we learned in the previous chapter, the Word of God does not fail. However, we receive the promise only if we place our complete trust in God's Word. The Word of God cautions us that if we waver in our faith, we forfeit the promises of God (see James 1:6-7).

At times we, too, may question God's Word. Unresolved doubt causes us to falter along the way, as in the case of Peter. However, when we falter, we must identify who or what is hindering us from walking in faith. People or circumstances can hinder us only if we lose focus on God's Word. If we understand Jesus' admonishment of Peter, we see that He simply identified his loss of focus. He was teaching Peter that His Word is greater than Peter's circumstances. Circumstances, by definition, change. However, God's Word stands the test of time. The more time we spend with God, the more opportunities He has to demonstrate His faithfulness. Much like a toddler, through experience, our walk of faith grows steady and secure.

While it is easy to point out that Peter faltered along the way, we must not overlook an important fact: Peter walked on water. To my knowledge, he is the only person aside from Jesus who is recorded as accomplishing this feat. This account is yet another example of the miraculous things we can accomplish when we give the Word of God preeminence in our lives. Even if we stumble along the way, we can still have assurance that we can accomplish great things through Christ Jesus.

Life is filled with trials and tests designed to strengthen your faith. Jesus promises that no matter what you go through, He is always with you (see Matt. 28:20). He is ahead of you when you need guidance, behind you when you need encouragement, and beside you when you need assistance. No matter what circumstances you find yourself in, He is never far from you. Take comfort in knowing that though you may falter, Jesus never fails. He is always there to extend a helping hand.

You'll Never Walk Alone

Recently, I witnessed something that gave new meaning to the term "walking by faith." I watched a documentary about a man who was physically blind. He'd lost his eyesight as a young boy and had spent most of his life with what we consider a disability. I was amazed as I listened to the interview. From a very young age, he'd learned to manage without the benefit of physical sight. It was amazing to see him conduct his daily chores. He'd learned that his footsteps made different sounds when he approached an opening or doorway. He'd developed a keen sense of smell, which he used to identify everything from food to medicine. He knew where everything was in his home and exactly how many steps it took him to get there. The biographer spent an entire day with him, and during that time the blind man cooked his own meals, shaved, and even played the piano. This man accomplished all of this without the assistance of people or devices. He didn't even use a cane. The man I speak of is none other than the musical legend Ray Charles.

The biographer working on the documentary was more amazed by Ray's ability to navigate his daily life than he was by his storied musical accomplishments. Ray, in a very mercurial way, told the biographer something I will never forget. "The reason you are impressed is because you think that I can't see," said Ray. "The truth is, I see just fine. I just see differently." As my writing for this book was drawing to a close, I couldn't help but think about what Ray said. I realized that Ray didn't need physical sight because he had learned to see through his mind's eye. Even though he could not physically see, he knew what was there. This vision that Ray possessed was operated by faith.

As I reflect on God's Word, I have a clearer perspective of walking by faith. I began this book by sharing my personal challenges as I've endeavored to walk by faith, and over time I've come to realize that my ability to walk by faith is inextricably linked to the way I view the world around me. As I have drawn closer to God, I have learned to see things from His point of view, which has given me the confidence and the strength to walk by faith.

Walking by faith does not imply that we won't stumble at times. It is quite the contrary. Allowing God to help us along the way, if and when we stumble, is what faith is all about. Jesus was anointed to, among other things, restore sight to the blind. I can truly say that I once was blind, but now I see. The truth of God's Word and the leading of His Spirit have changed my perspective. This change of view or spiritual vision, in turn, enables me to walk by faith. I too have learned to see differently. Even though I can't see Jesus with my natural eyes, I know that He's with me. Be strong in the Lord, knowing that He is with you also. When you exercise *Ridiculous Faith*, you'll never walk alone.

EPILOGUE

No matter how hard I tried, I couldn't fall asleep. The idea that had impregnated my mind had taken hold and would not be subdued by slumber. I had no recourse but to explore the idea further.

I had an overwhelming desire to begin work on a book manuscript. The idea was not totally foreign. From my early childhood, I had had aspirations of becoming an author, and as an adolescent, I had completed a number of literary works including poems, essays, and a children's book. Few pursuits provided the joy that writing gave me. It was also an important avenue for creativity and expression that developed my self-esteem.

As I progressed through high school and college, my childhood dreams died, however. At least it seemed that way to me. They were sacrificed on the altar that we call reality. I was told that it wasn't rational to pursue a career as an author—writers don't earn any money. Your time should be dedicated to more prudent undertakings. Childhood dreams are simply the preoccuppation of children...or are they? As I lay in bed that fateful night, I realized that childhood dreams don't really die. In a sense they are buried alive—buried under a mountain of worry about family, finances, career, and the cares of life. Maybe it was time my dream was resurrected.

In July 2001, my lovely wife, Latania, and I traveled to Spain on vacation. We didn't have children at the time and were both in the midst of demanding careers. She was working as a manager and senior consultant at a leading consulting firm, and I worked in sales at an investment banking firm. We both worked long hours and traveled extensively, so it was great to have the opportunity to take a break. My career seemed to be in high gear, having literally gone from Chicago's main streets to New York's Wall Street. Although I was quite comfortable with my life, it was about to be thrown into a tailspin.

As I was musing over the prospect of writing a book, God spoke to me. It's hard for many people to accept that God actually speaks to people. Life conditions us to be skeptics. However, I had no doubt in my mind that I'd heard from God. It was not an audible voice per se, yet I could hear the voice in my thoughts as if God were seated next to the bed. As my wife remained sound asleep, God said to me, "You want to write; so go ahead and write!" Some might think that doesn't sound very profound, but the key was that it was prophetic. God personally spoke to me concerning my life, and it was expressed in a way that I easily understood.

I'd love to tell you that there was more to the experience than that. However, that was the extent of our interaction. There was no miraculous event and no fantastic vision. We didn't even have a conversation. God didn't tell me what to write about. He didn't tell me when to start. He didn't promise me that I'd be commercially successful as an author or that I'd get published for that matter. He simply affirmed what was in my heart for as long as I could remember. God had given me both the ability and desire to produce literary works. The only thing standing in the way was my lack of faith.

I immediately got out of bed and grabbed a pad and pen from the hotel nightstand. I feverishly began to scribble notes well into the wee hours of the night. Those notes became the genesis for my first book project, *Stop Digging! and Start Planting!* When I finally fell asleep, I had a strange sense of excitement. All I had was a title, an outline, and some jumbled notes, but there was a hint of change in the air. I had no idea that one restless night, a colorful idea, and a simple Word from God would dramatically change my life.

When I returned to Chicago, I was excited about the prospect of working on the book, and as I began to further develop my idea for the book, I realized I would need to expand it into two separate volumes. I invited one my oldest and dearest friends to collaborate with me on the project, and we eventually decided to independently publish the books. We started our own publishing press and moved into the retailing side of the business by acquiring a Christian bookstore. The undertaking became so consuming that we left our lucrative investment jobs to make the dream a reality.

I'd love to tell you that we met with overwhelming commercial success, but that wasn't the case. During the next couple years, I experienced many life changes and many challenges. First, I was blessed with the birth of my two beautiful sons, Javon and Micah. Then, in a short period of time our family went from having two comfortable incomes to no income at all. The businesses were burning cash while we were doing all we could to establish them and reach profitability. This lack of income and other unexpected circumstances depleted our savings over time. The book project went well in retrospect, but it underperformed our expectations and more importantly underperformed our financial commitments to the project.

As the situation evolved, I began to question myself. *Should I give up on writing? Was it all in vain? Had I actually heard from God?* That's when it happened again. God spoke to me another time. His message this time was about much more than my literary or business pursuits. "You exercise very little faith," He told me. It wasn't quite the encouraging words I wanted to hear, but it was a vital word that came at a critical time in my life.

God began to show me how I spent much of my life worrying needlessly—worry that prevented me from enjoying a closer relationship with Him. Although I thought I understood faith, I hadn't been relying on Him. Through my experience with the book project, He did more than reignite a childhood dream; the process stripped away many of the things that I'd unconsciously relied on—my finances, my job, and even my friends. I was able reevaluate my perspective of faith. In a sense, I was able to start over.

From that point, the Spirit began to reveal to me what faith in God was really about. I would later coin the term *Ridiculous Faith*.

There was a constant chorus of questions as I made decisions along my personal journey of faith: Why do you want to write books? Why are you qualified? Why did you quit a lucrative job? Why did you purchase a floundering retail business? To that constant chorus of whys, I simply say, "Why not? Why not me? Why not this? Why not now?" The Bible tells us that God searches the earth looking for people to show His might through. He has destined everyone for greatness, but faith in Him is required to get there. The excerise of faith provides the opportunity, but not the gurantee, that God will accomplish the miraculous through my life. If you want to know my philosophy concerning faith, it's quite simple—I want to afford God that opportunity.

God is faithful and He has proven Himself to me. Our business eventually reached profitability, and we believe that it will continue to flourish. I have a new job at an outstanding firm. Moreover, the job content and work enviroment are a good personal fit. This book is the fruit of my personal journey of faith. People have questioned my decision to continue writing; nevertheless, God has opened several doors, and several entities have been interested in the manuscript. I'm grateful that God has afforded me the ability and the privilege of writing. I am also grateful for every opportunity I have to testify of His grace. Faith is what sustains me as I endeavor to make a meaningful contribution to the human experience. *Ridiculous Faith* is what resurrected my dream of becoming an author and more importantly secured my relationship with God. I pray that this book has strengthened your faith. I also pray that God restores the dreams of your youth. Faith is your key for unlocking the destiny that God has especially for you, and Jesus Christ is the author and finisher of your faith.

Therefore, since we are surrounded by such a huge crowd of witnesses to the life of faith, let us strip off every weight that slows us down, especially the sin that so easily hinders our progress. And let us run with endurance the race that God has set before us. We do this by keeping our eyes on Jesus, on whom our faith depends from start to finish. He was willing to die a shameful death on the cross because of the joy He knew would be His afterward. Now He is seated in the place of highest honor beside God's throne in heaven. Think about all He endured when sinful people did such terrible things to Him, so that you don't become weary and give up (Hebrews 12:1-3 NLT).

ABOUT THE AUTHOR

Shundrawn A. Thomas, a native and resident of Chicago, Illinois, is a gifted teacher, author, counselor, entrepreneur, husband, and father. A licensed minister and motivational speaker, Shundrawn tirelessly uses his ministry gifts to empower and encourage individuals in the areas of faith, family and finance.

Professionally, Shundrawn serves as Head of Corporate Strategy for The Northern Trust Company, a leading wealth management and asset servicing firm. He previously served as a vice president for Goldman Sachs, a premiere investment banking firm. As a senior relationship manager, he advised some of the world's largest institutional equity investors. His principled business approach and dedication to excellence have made him an invaluable advisor to institutions and individuals.

Shundrawn is an entrepreneur, serving as co-founder of Adelphos Holdings LLC. The company's primary business is Christian retail operating under the SincereMilk brand name. Shundrawn and his wife are also the proprietors of another enterprise—Tree of Life Resources LLP which develops faith-based multi-media content.

Shundrawn is very involved in his local church and community. He serves as a minister and board member of Look Up and Live Full Gospel Ministries. His church and community activism have afforded him numerous opportunities to speak locally and nationally on subjects including Christian living, faith, marriage, education, entrepreneurship, and personal finance.

Shundrawn holds a Bachelor of Science in accounting from Florida A&M University. He holds a Masters of Business Administration from the University of Chicago's Graduate School of Business. Shundrawn is happily married and enjoys spending time with his wife, Latania, and their sons, Javon and Micah.

FOR MORE INFORMATION

To find out more information about Shundrawn A. Thomas, his mission and his message, visit

www.RidiculousFaith.com

Get news about his upcoming projects.
Request him as a speaker at your special event.
Share your testimony of ridiculous faith.
Spread the message to family and friends.